Faith and Sexism

Faith and Sexism

Guidelines for Religious Educators

Marianne Sawicki

A Crossroad Book
THE SEABURY PRESS • NEW YORK

1979
The Seabury Press
815 Second Avenue, New York, N.Y. 10017

Design by Charlette Bundy
Printed in the United States of America

Library of Congress Cataloging in Publication Data

Sawicki, Marianne.
    Faith and Sexism
    "A Crossroad book."
1. Sexism in Christian education.
2. Christian education and language.
3. Christian education—Text-books—Catholic.
4. Sex (Theology)   I. Title.
BV1464.S28   268'.6   79-5176

ISBN: 0-8164-0105-5

The author gratefully acknowledges the input of those who
collaborated in the genesis of these guidelines:

Eileen Anderson	Janaan Manternach
Margrit Banta	Berard L. Marthaler
Dorothy Bock	Edward Murray
Janet Brink	Joseph Nangle
William Callahan	Michelle Olley
Elizabeth Carroll	Dolly Pomerleau
Robert Duford	Patricia Rengel
Nadine Foley	Joseph Slattery
Virgil Funk	Marie Spellacy
Francis Gignac	Arlene Swidler
Robert Hovda	Leonard Swidler
Dolores Leckey	Paul Zomberg

CONTENTS

PROLOGUE

Jesus Christ reveals to us who God is, and who we are. This revelation comes to us in the words of the Bible and in tradition. Because the catechizing Church continues to interpret the word of God in light of changing historical circumstances, the Christian revelation can continue to happen for each individual in every age. There is a revelatory dimension in every human life that makes each of us able to receive the gift of God's life, given once and for all in Jesus.

The word of God remains unchanged, but its meaning unfolds in dialogue with human concerns in an evolving world. The question of the status of women, which has emerged with great urgency in our society, can be put to the word of God in Sacred Scripture. A theology of the sexes is to be found in the books of the Bible, expressed in the mytho-symbolic language characteristic of the ancient texts.

The Book of Genesis says that God originally intended the sexes to have equal status. The New Testament gives the reason: both sexes share the destiny of union with God in Christ. In the time between the Creation and the Parousia, however, sin disrupts the harmony between the sexes by introducing exploitative relationships and systematic oppression. Jesus, the savior who has overcome the alienation between human beings, teaches a new dignity for both women and men.

In Jesus Christ God has inaugurated a new age and a new

reign on earth. In this reign the equal status of the sexes is restored, even though the effects of sin still linger and hamper Christians as they work for the reign of God. Whatever the difficulties we encounter in the present day, we are assured that God's word has been spoken on behalf of justice for the sexes. This word has the power to accomplish what it has promised.

God's word is heard always in human words. The inspired words of Scripture express more than the eternal truths of salvation; indirectly they tell us about the time and place in which they were written as well as the concerns of their human authors. There are other words of God besides Scripture. Each Christian is a word of God to others. The Church is a word of God to the world. Catechesis is a word of God addressed to the ecclesial community. None of these words is a perfect word or a last word, for they are human words with intrinsic limitations. None of them taken alone can ever be the best possible expression of God's saving act in Jesus Christ.

The utterances of human beings characteristically reflect the sinfulness of the world in which they are situated. While the Church's magisterium has never spoken falsely about Jesus, the Church does speak of him in more and more adequate ways as history goes on. As the Church continues its theological reflection on the gospel and as it strives to live out God's word more faithfully through the guidance of the Holy Spirit, the Church speaks more truly of Jesus and presents his message more comprehensively and more accurately.

In this century the Church is realizing how thoroughly its catechesis can become saturated with elements of the sinful world order. The Church's message is susceptible to such an admixture because the Church is a human entity on the way to the reign of God as well as a divinely instituted symbol of that reign. As the Church becomes aware of the adulteration of its message, it gains the perspective it needs to correct it. Lately the Church in the United States has realized that it can take steps to eliminate one contaminating element, the influence of sexism, from catechesis.

There are several reasons for this new awareness. Sexist discrimination is incompatible with the essence of Jesus' teachings. The gospel itself overturns sexist attitudes and subverts sexist structures. The salvation which Jesus brings is for *all* people. The development of the sciences involved in scriptural exegesis now makes it possible to separate elements arising out of the time, place, and concerns of the writers of the biblical books from the inspired message they sought to convey. Modern exegesis can peel away layers of androcentric (male-centered) language and misogynist (anti-woman) attitudes to expose the meaning of the word of God with greater clarity than ever before.

Catechesis must be undertaken in a spirit of obedience to the revelation given in Jesus Christ, a spirit of concern for the Church and its rising generations, and a spirit of joyful thanksgiving for our own liberation from sin (which is as yet incomplete). The Bible is normative for all catechesis and for the present guidelines. Twenty centuries of Christian tradition help to interpret the Bible, but this tradition itself also needs interpretation. Present experience and the practical dictates of pedagogical science and common sense control how Scripture and tradition are presented effectively to Christians of all ages.

Catechetical Goals

Catechesis is an ecclesial activity whose goal is that Christians and their communities grow in faith. Growing faith becomes more and more conscious of itself, and becomes more deliberately active in expressing what it believes. Faith expresses itself in relationships with God, with one's neighbor, and with oneself.

Catechesis toward justice for the sexes has objectives in each of these three dimensions of the faith relationship. First, it aims to bring Christians to fuller knowledge and love of God by explaining the symbolic language and the metaphors in which God is described. No image is adequate to express the being of God, yet we have no way to speak of God except with metaphors — taken from Scripture and the Christian tradition or devised anew. These figures of speech surely hide as much as they disclose, and must be used with care. The full range of metaphors which the Bible applies to God should be explored to get the fullest possible idea of what God is like. These inadequate words *about* God also give us the words with which we speak *to* God. Catechesis leads Christians to address God in

3

prayer under the variety of images in which God has addressed us. In the pages of Scripture, God's love overflows in a wealth of analogues drawn from all kinds of human loving relations. Human hearts respond with love to the many images, both male and female, in which God's love is symboled to us.

Secondly, growing faith expresses itself in more just and more loving relationships with the neighbor. Catechesis toward justice for the sexes points out the exploitative and oppressive social structures which diminish the human potential of both men and women. It teaches people to resist the coercive power of stereotyped roles for the sexes in their own interpersonal relationships. Catechesis helps faith grow by calling for personal conversion away from the sexist attitudes that stand in the way of our seeing Christ in other people.

Finally, growing faith expresses itself in more peaceful acceptance of one's self and the strengths and weaknesses one has been given by God. Catechesis fosters self-esteem in both sexes. It helps Christians to integrate the entire range of Christian virtues in their lives. It makes clear to both sexes their equal responsibility to develop their talents and to use them for the reign of God.

Sharing the Light of Faith

The new National Catechetical Directory, *Sharing the Light of Faith*, mandates catechesis toward justice for the sexes and situates it in the tradition of Catholic moral teaching. Respect for human life and the dignity of the person are two foundational themes in *Sharing the Light of Faith*. Basic human rights and duties arise directly from our common humanity, regardless of sex (#157). Human dignity demands that the person's spiritual, psychological, emotional, and bodily integrity be respected (#156). This statement stands as a warning not to bring stereotypical role expectations to bear upon either sex. Today we see that such oppression and manipulation, however subtle or well-intentioned, runs contrary to the gospel. The respect which is due life is "violated in attempts to hamper another's capacity to live as fully as possible, or to reduce a person to a state of dependency" (#167). Injustice may have its roots in personal sin or in social sin, but all who recognize it have the moral responsibility to seek to correct it (#165).

Sharing the Light of Faith points out that sin has both personal and social consequences. Among sin's effects, the Directory lists exploitative relationships, unjust social structures and policies, the oppression of the weak and the manipulation of the vulnerable (#98). These things show that sin is a reality in the world, involving systematic abuse of the rights of certain groups and individuals (#165). Morality, too, has a social dimension, and the Church's moral teaching serves as a guide for social morality as well as for personal morality (#158). Catechesis must foster a renewal of heart and lifelong conversion away from injustice. It must help Christians recognize their obligations to overcome personal and social sin, and their inability to do so by their own power (#170).

There can be no conversion and no moral action at all without freedom. Catechesis cannot make anyone free. It simply removes obstacles to the full enjoyment of the freedom that God gives us as a constituent of our human nature. The Directory points out that true morality "is not something imposed from without; rather, it is the way people accept their humanity as restored to them in Christ" (#102). Sexuality remains part of that restored humanity. Catechesis should show the dignity of maleness and femaleness in order to help men and women accept their own God-given sexual identity and their relatedness to other people. Both femaleness and maleness endow the person with equal potential for full humanity, for imitation of Christ, and for status in the reign of God. Catechesis provides young people with examples of both women and men who have made worthwhile contributions to the community. Using these models, young people can frame their own aspirations to sanctity and service. Knowing the full range of human possibility, they are enabled to choose a lifestyle and a career freely. Catechesis encourages both sexes to follow Christ in the practice of the virtues, the beatitudes, and the works of mercy.

Catechesis toward justice for the sexes is not just another item in the curriculum to be added on to Bible study, the sacraments, moral instruction, social teaching, the lives of the saints, and the other elements of the Christian message. Rather, it permeates all the other elements. Sacramental, moral, doctrinal, and biblical catechesis are all affected by it; they must all present positive images of the sexes and further the goal of justice for the sexes. This is so because sexuality is essential to humanity, not accidental to it. Sexuality is at issue in everything that has to do with human beings.

The Christian message addresses persons in their concrete human situation, a situation in which sexuality is an irreducible factor. Every part of the message has relevance for women and men and their relationships. Because of this fact, the present guidelines embrace the Christian message in its entirety. They have something to say to each of the ten categories of catechesis listed in Chapter V of *Sharing the Light of Faith*. Since these guidelines follow the same order of presentation, they can be easily used along with the Directory. An eleventh category lists items that have to do with the process of catechesis rather than the message itself.

Christ at the Center

Christ *is* the gospel's message. Catechesis is Christocentric, and everything it has to say about human beings is said in light of their redemption by the coming of the Christ.

Both sexes find in Jesus an example, someone who fulfilled his own (male) sexuality and overcame its limitations. Jesus' manhood gave him access to the full range of human experience and expression. A human being like us in everything but sin, he knew some human realities by directly experiencing them — sonship, hope, learning, hunger, disappointment, fatigue, amusement, friendship, death. There were other realities in which Jesus did not directly participate, but which he was able to understand humanly through compassion, empathy, intuition, and identification with the experiences of the people close to him — among these would be marriage, old age, fatherhood, motherhood. Jesus, like other human beings of broad understanding and great poetic skill, communicated effectively with people of both sexes. He expressed God's boundless love by using metaphors and analogues drawn from the experiences of both sexes. In his active ministry he violated the rigid role stereotypes and social divisions between the sexes that existed in his world. Conceptually he overturned the male viewpoint of the Torah, the Prophets and the Wisdom literature. For the sake of the reign of God, Jesus transcended the limitations of his own maleness in his poetic logic, his deeds, and his doctrine.

The reality of Christ today overcomes all divisions, including that which divides the sexes. While one may still think of the risen, glorified body of Jesus as a male body — insofar as Jesus retains his own individual human identity, a male identity — nevertheless the ecclesial and eucharistic body of Christ is without sex. Both men and women are drawn to Christ and see their destiny in the Risen Christ. Both sexes are redeemed by Christ and both sexes imitate Christ. All of human reality is taken up in Christ, who gives each man and woman today the possibility of fulfilling his or her own sexual identity while overcoming its limitations.

Jesus Christ is the Lord who has overcome the world and its sinful structures. This is a message of hope which catechesis should deliver whenever it discusses the sin of sexism and its effects. Jesus himself taught that both women and men have new status in the reign of God. Jesus chose women to bear the good news of salvation to others, for he judged their words worthy to become evangelizing words of God. The Eucharist, which expresses symbolically Jesus' self-understanding and his salvific sacrifice, resonates with the feminine Yahweh imagery of the Hebrew Scriptures and with the experiences of women and men in every age.

The Importance of Language

The medium of catechesis is human language, especially the spoken word. If catechesis is to be true to the gospel of Jesus Christ, it must use language that expresses Jesus' teaching about the equal dignity of each person. Language is of crucial importance in every human activity: in coming to understand, in planning for the future, in grasping one's own identity, and in relating to other people. We easily manipulate language, yet our everyday ways of speaking manipulate us too. Some brief reflections on the nature of language may help to explain why using the right words is essential to achieving justice for the sexes.

Sexuality is an essential characteristic of every human being. The same thing can be said of language: it is no mere possession but rather the fullest embodiment of being human. Both the body and language have their limits. The confinement of our language and our particular sexual identity seem to be a necessary part of this world. We are possessed of language; language possesses us. Language expresses the person, just as the body expresses the person. Language, like the body, presents to the individual every possibility which she or he has vis-a-vis the world, while it simultaneously imposes the limitations which constrain our commerce with social and material reality.

Because they are foundational for our world, both language and sexual differentiation are shattered and at the same time fulfilled and transcended as Jesus inaugurates the reign of God. To say that Christ transcends sexual differentiation and overcomes the limits of language is to make an eschatological affirmation, a statement of faith that the reign of God is upon us even though we do not perceive it and cannot describe its meaning.

Language gives us possession of whatever we possess. To name something is to have it; we do not own what we cannot name. To name is to control, for in naming we assign things to categories wherein they are easy to handle. Naming exorcises mystery and imposes predictability upon what is named. The named can be called up and dispatched; it can be given away, retained, destroyed, consumed, or changed into something else. Naming can be a loving or a hateful act, a gift of identity or an annihilation through ridicule.

The concept is a kind of name, inhabiting the mind before coming to utterance. Connotation surrounds a name with notions of the purpose, utility, value, relatedness, and intentionality of the thing named. We think with concepts: we add and subtract them, we associate them with other concepts in order to disclose possibilities for ourselves and for the objects named. Over time, concepts are built up in the mind through many transactions in language. We develop concepts corresponding to different things in the world, to possible ways of acting in the world, to other people, and to ourselves. The self-concept is the most treasured of all.

Just as we do not know things we have not named, we cannot choose to do something for which we have no concept. We need models. What other people do and say gives us examples that disclose possibilities for our own doing. As we pick up names and concepts linguistically from other people, we learn about our own possibilities from the way in which others speak to us and about us.

Moreover, language itself is the repository of the meanings, namings, conceptualizations, and aspirations of all who have lived until now. It is a universe; what is unknown in language cannot be part of the world where we dwell together. The possibilities of language are vast but finite, and they circumscribe the space in which we live. Language is a given, and is possessed of a common-sense wisdom which we call the "everybody says." Names and concepts expressed in the common language have the force of consensus, for all speakers agree upon what the terms mean. This mighty language is nevertheless something which we hold in common, and something which holds us. Language is our most commonly used tool, ever ready to serve and to be adapted for better service.

Yet, language exerts a certain power over all human reality. A pronoun, tiny as it is, maps out the entire field of human relationships, marking off the borders of "we," "they," "you." Once these lines are set, all further elaborations of the various human relations takes place within them, never across them. There are endless varieties of "we" — there is marriage, partnership in business, friendship, casual encounter, nationhood, and so on. But none of those is "I." "Thou" can be many shades of relationship, but only within the limits already laid down by language at the dawn of human linguistic being. The one who is called "thou" will cease to be so when called "he." Our language has pronouns that connote personal being of indefinite gender in the first and second persons and in the third person plural (I, you, we, they), but lacks a pronoun that is personal, singular, and genderless in the third person (there are only he, she, and it).

Such limitations are intrinsic to language. It cannot say everything. Its capacity for expansion is circumscribed, for while it can go on naming new things and developing new concepts indefinitely, it cannot overcome its most basic categories. Rather, it cannot overcome them *literally* but does indeed transcend them through the use of metaphor and related figures of speech. Poetry knows ways to break the logical law of non-contradiction. The metaphor achieves its meaning precisely by casting a familiar concept into a new and incongruous context. If the metaphor works, a new congruity emerges and meaning is expressed which could not have been said literally and which cannot be translated into ordinary talk. Metaphor deliberately breaks the rules of literal logic and oversteps the bounds of language's basic categories. Its semantic is odd but entirely valid. It is an event of meaning which in time can cease to happen and become stale.

Much biblical language uses metaphor and other figures of speech. We may assume that the scriptural writers were aware of what they were doing. They insist that there can be no images of God in stone, metal, or wood, but then they find numerous images of God in poetic words. They insist that God is without sex, but then they propose analogues of both sexes to describe God. The images and analogues often are incompatible with each other if they are taken literally; for example, a nursing mother cannot be the same being as a jealous husband. Therefore, these metaphors for God are *not* to be taken literally. Each one contributes some figurative meaning to our understanding of God. We need the whole range of biblical images if we are to begin to get some idea of what God is like.

Language confines human beings as well. Each individual has her or his own name. Unfortunately, it is all too easy to ignore that fact and to deal conceptually with individuals by assigning them to categories. These categories, or stereotypes, save us the trouble of discovering the unique characteristics of each human being. Thinking in stereotypes is lazy thinking. Sex–role stereotyping is one of the most pernicious and widespread varieties. Sex stereotyping substitutes the term "woman" or "man" for the person's own name. It sees the category instead of the individual, and often misjudges the category as well. Most of all, sex stereotyping denies one the benefit of having others look for the unpredictable, the novel, the original, the extraordinary in one's behavior. When others expect nothing unusual, it is hard to disappoint them. The socially assigned sex role, pervading all communication, seeps into the person's mind and displaces the individual self-concept. Nothing rivals ridicule in its power to reduce the humanity and individuality of the person. When one hears, "A typical woman!" or, "I couldn't expect a man to understand," one's sense of one's own uniqueness and promise simply shrivels up. As we once accepted the gift of our individual name from our parents, and along with it the promise of a unique identity and destiny, so we are prone to accept the names which others give, even when they violate our individuality and humanity.

People need help to resist the coercive power of the names society assigns to them. Catechesis can give such help. It fosters growth in freedom. It affirms the individual's own worth, potential, uniqueness, and destiny. It can do so because Jesus is a new language and Christ is our new name. Jesus is the word of obedience and acceptance who receives his identity from God. He discloses to men and women who they really are. Because of Jesus' obedience and receptivity, God has given him the name above every other name. Jesus, the new language, asserts his lordship over all human reality and displaces the meanings which everything had before. The gospel is a new story, good news proclaimed to women and men alike.

Change Is Difficult

The gospel sets its own precedent for overturning traditional language and subverting accustomed roles. Jesus dared to speak to God as Abba, or Dad, an outrageous form of address in a culture where one did not even pronounce the name of the deity. Catechesis today does not come on with the suddenness of Jesus' proclamation, of course. For us, catechesis is a lifelong affair, and at best the conversion of heart is gradual and steady. The Christ comes into our lives little by little and the change is hardly noticeable, or so it usually seems. Yet any change is difficult. This is especially so when it means a change in language, which is so intimately connnected with our identity and our everyday working assumptions and attitudes.

Nothing changes without a change in language. Conversion from sin and alteration of sin's social effects must express themselves in language. Many of sin's effects are linguistic disruptions, so surely this is a good place to start. Catechists must learn to say, "Christ died to save all men and women." Not only is this a truer proclamation, but in addition it piques sexist expectations by jolting the listener who is accustomed to hear just "all men." Patience and compassion are still in order, however, for the gospel without sexism is a hard thing to listen to.

Sensitive catechists will know how to achieve a balance

between the old words and the new, sliding in the new words and easing out the old. Change is not easy. However, it is possible — indeed, it should be more possible for Christians than for others, since Christianity means conversion. Changing the language of catechesis may at first seem revolutionary, but it is more properly termed evolutionary. Catechesis toward justice for the sexes represents a logical development of our understanding of the gospel.

The change of catechetical language required by the goal of justice for the sexes is a change altogether in line with the tradition. No radical alteration of the Christian symbol system is needed. Rather, there must be a recovery of the full meaning of the Christian symbols as the Bible presents them. Every suggestion made in these guidelines arises from insights expressed in Scripture. One need not look outside revelation to find images of equality between the sexes, or non-masculine analogues for the loving care of God. The essentials are there in the word of God. The gospel is the sole motive behind these guidelines as they aim to bring about a more complete understanding of what Christians have always believed, and a fuller participation in its reality.

Two Paradoxes

It is hard to decide where to begin with catechesis toward justice for the sexes. Paradoxically, the logical point of departure is also the goal at which catechesis is aiming: knowledge of who God is and who human beings are. If we could settle upon an image of God and an image of the person, then it would be relatively simple to draw up rules for speaking about both. But the identity of God remains a mystery despite thousands of years of theological reflection on revelation. Moreover, we do not have all the data on which to decide the identity of the human being; we do not know yet who we might turn out to be. There are question marks in place of images at the two possible starting points for catechesis.

This paradox is compounded by a second in the case of the present guidelines. These guidelines take published materials as their principal target — or rather, materials that are now being written for publication. Yet materials are only a secondary element in catechesis; catechists themselves are the most important and influential component of the catechetical enterprise. Therefore, these guidelines also must address catechists, youth ministers, ministers of adult education, and the directors of the programs who train such personnel.

The whole Church is a catechist. Moreover, the whole Church is a textbook for catechesis. This means that the *primary agent* of catechesis and the major *content* of catechesis both lie beyond the direct influence of these guidelines.

The National Catechetical Directory analyzes what has traditionally been called "content" into four kinds of "signs." Instead of teaching some content, catechesis is said to interpret four signs: biblical, liturgical, ecclesial, and natural. Their content is already determined before the catechist encounters them. If they contain sexist elements, catechesis must give them an interpretation that is faithful to the gospel.

Biblical signs are the stories, prayers, laws, advice, admonition, promises, etc., in Sacred Scripture, which is the primary source for all catechesis. So close is the association between the word of God and Scripture that the term "revelation" has been used as a synonym for "Bible." The catechetical task with regard to Scripture is not to change its words, but to understand exactly what is being said in every verse, on every page. *Liturgical signs* are the words and gestures of the liturgy. Many liturgical words come from Scripture or elaborate upon it. Catechesis aims at greater understanding of the liturgy and participation in it. In addition, catechesis interprets liturgy to disclose to Christians the character of their relationship with God. *Ecclesial signs* include texts such as creeds and Church pronouncements, as well as the entire witness of the Christian lifestyle. These words and this example are powerful catechising influences. *Natural signs* embrace all that is going on in the world and in the Church today, everything that belongs to the culture, everyday life, and present human experience of the people.

These guidelines can do nothing to affect the "content" of any of the four signs, but catechists and textbook writers can influence how people understand that content. Because catechesis is interpretation, catechists can lead people to more mature and nuanced understanding. Therefore, these guidelines honestly call attention to the androcentrism, misogyny, and sexist stereotypes that appear in the four signs of catechesis, with a view to helping catechists deal creatively with these negative elements. Catechists should see to it that the gospel's clear demand for justice for the sexes drowns out the sexist overtones in the rest of the Bible and in the tradition as it has developed since biblical times.

It is advisable for catechists to cultivate a sense of history and to use it when they deal with texts that come down to us from the past. Such texts, whether they be scriptural or not, constitute a precious heritage. They are handed down to us wrapped in layers of historic interpretation. Thanks to modern exegetical techniques, historical research, and philological studies, we are better prepared today than ever before to recover the meaning of these texts as it was meant in the time and the culture in which they were written. Catechesis can succeed only when it is absolutely faithful to the meaning and the spirit of the texts which it interprets. Catechesis toward justice for the sexes will succeed to the extent that it is a faithful interpretation of the gospel.

Texts from out of the past also interpret one another. The Christian Scriptures interpret the Hebrew Scriptures (which is why they have been called the New Testament and the Old Testament, respectively). The writers of Christian antiquity interpret both testaments. Later magisterial pronouncements of the Church add their own layers of interpretation. The liturgy itself interprets the Scripture and Christian experience. These layers of interpretation which enable the word of God to reach us today are to be respected. However, they remain subordinate to the original meaning of the words of Scripture, to the extent that it can be recovered through sound exegesis. A proper understanding of the role of theological and liturgical interpretation down through history brings these interpretations to life again and lets them do the work they are written to do. Within the bounds of the best interpretive scholarship — and indeed because of what it discloses about the Christian message — non-sexist catechesis gives texts from the past a creative handling that helps the meaning of the gospel to speak to women and men in our day.

Professionals Who Might Use These Guidelines

Catechists stand at the end of a long line of people who have interpreted the gospel, and they in turn hand on the message to those whom they catechize. Usually catechists rely on printed materials specially written to bring the word of God to the age group they are addressing. Textbook writers and publishers, too, are therefore involved in the catechetical endeavor, along with the parish and diocesan directors of religious education who select catechetical materials and recruit and train catechists. All of these professional people — catechists, directors of religious education, youth ministers, ministers of adult education, campus ministry staffs, diocesan directors, writers, and publishers — should find these guidelines helpful.

Most publishing houses already have their own guidelines for presenting positive images of the sexes in secular textbooks. Many publishers have found it difficult to apply these to religion texts. A Christian religion textbook seeks to introduce the Christian symbols, but these symbols taken at face value seem to be intrinsically sexist. For example, even in the fundamental doctrine of the Trinity, two of the three Persons have male names. The Christian message, wrapped in its layers of historical interpretation, does present certain special problems that math, geography and spelling do not. These problems can be solved, but publishers need some special theological advice for handling them. These guidelines seek to fill that need by helping publishers adapt their own general guidelines to religion textbooks. In addition, these guidelines alert religious education directors and catechists to some factors they should consider in selecting a textbook series.

The catechizing Church has its own reasons for enthusiastically endorsing the guidelines that have already been developed for secular textbooks. One basic premise supports secular publishers' and educators' efforts to eliminate sex-role stereotyping from textbooks: sexism is a mistake in logic. Sexism is based on the mistaken assumption that certain physical characteristics can predict the personality, behavior, and destiny of individuals. This mistake in logic impedes the smooth functioning of society because it keeps human resources from being used to their fullest potential. Overspecialization of the sexes in rigidly defined roles leads to social waste. From a humanistic perspective, sexism is unjust and injustice ought to be eradicated wherever possible. This argument gives the secular publisher sufficient reason for seeking to represent both sexes fairly in textbooks.

For the Christian textbook writer, sexism is more than social waste. It is sin. It is anti–gospel. It goes against the reign of God. The Christian creed says that salvation in Christ is for everyone. Jesus Christ has overcome sexism along with all other sin. The gospel gives Christians a mandate to resist sin, and the means to eliminate it. Christians must witness to the liberation which they teach and let their lifestyle embody it. With the publication of the National Catechetical Directory, the Catholic Church in the United States has officially thrown its weight behind catechesis toward justice for the sexes.

Christians have one supreme model, one "stereotype," who is the Christ. Any socially contrived stereotype that rivals Christ is idolatrous. In essence, this is the element which Christian catechesis adds to the guidelines already being used in many publishing houses. The gospel not only demands that sexism be eliminated, but will be powerfully instrumental in that elimination as well.

The message of liberation from sexism is for everyone in the Church, but these guidelines have as their primary concern future generations who will be using the textbooks now being written. These young people are forming ideas of themselves and their place in the world. They are aspiring to use their talents in careers they will be choosing. They need to see images of a world where each person is welcomed because of her or his own dignity, and is enabled to develop her or his potential for the good of society. Young people need images in which to imagine the reign of God.

Catechesis toward justice for the sexes aims to nurture a generation who will grow up never suspecting that little girls might be worth less than little boys, never understanding the perverse logic of sex stereotypes that was taken for granted within our own memories. Perhaps these very guidelines will sound marvelously archaic to Christians of the twenty–first century who may happen to read them. It is to be hoped that those people will have no other exposure to our sin of sexism.

This prologue has introduced the major theological and philosophical arguments supporting the rest of the guidelines. In the eighty–five points that follow, the arguments are reinforced by Scriptural citations, applied to various contexts, and illustrated with examples. The theology of these guidelines is not an end unto itself. Rather, its purpose is to lay the foundation for some practical suggestions for catechetical programs and materials. Although these guidelines emerge from prayerful reflection on the gospel and the signs of the times by many knowledgeable people, they remain provisional in character and advisory in intent.

Marianne Sawicki
General Editor of
Liturgical Conference

GUIDELINES

The Mystery of the One God

1. **God — He or She?** God is neither male nor female, but spirit. Catechesis must emphasize that God is the fullness of being, without division. Both mystics and philosophers of language remind us that it is a mistake to speak of God in the third person at all, for God is always "thou" to us. Avoid pronouns whenever possible by repeating "God" or "God's." As an alternative, follow the example of Scripture and use terms like:

the finger of God,	the name of God,
the word of God,	the voice of God,
the glory of God,	the breath of God.

These phrases retain the sense of personhood, but they can be used with the neuter pronoun. In addition, they evoke a tone of mystery. As a last resort to avoid clumsy or distracting construction, the masculine singular pronoun is acceptable in historical or doctrinal material to refer to "God," "Yahweh," or "the Lord." In material that draws upon the feminine poetic imagery of Yahweh in the Hebrew Scripture, the femine pronoun may be the appropriate form. The problem of God's gender can be made the topic of a catechetical discussion or lesson.

2. **"Father."** This is the name which Jesus chose to express the character of God's relationship to him and to us. Jesus taught us to pray to God as Father, and Christian prayer has used the term ever since. Therefore, the name "Father" may appear often and prominently in textbooks. The qualities which it connotes are love, wisdom, the giving of life, and continued care. Other human relationships also embody these qualities, and can therefore be used as analogues to explain and enrich the idea of the fatherhood of God. Remember that some children have unfortunate experiences of their fathers, and the father role can carry unhealthy psychological associations. It is therefore essential to expand and explore the concept of God's parenthood by suggesting that God cares for us like a mother, like a grandfather, like a big sister, or even like a faithful daughter cares for her aged parent. Encourage discussion of the appropriateness of the father metaphor and other suitable metaphors for God.

GOD REMAINS "OUR FATHER," BUT WE ENRICH THIS NAME AND EXPLORE THE SUPERLATIVE DEGREE OF GOD'S PARENTHOOD BY USING A RANGE OF ANALOGUES, INCLUDING FEMALE RELATIVES.

3. **Images of God.** Although Scripture insists that God cannot really be pictured, it describes God in an amazing variety of poetic images. Added one to another, these metaphors cumulatively introduce us to our God. Each depicts another aspect of the ineffable. They teach us how to speak about God and to God. The Bible gives us both masculine and feminine metaphors in abundance, although none of these is really "correct" because God is without sex. To speak of God at all, we must use these sex–specific images while acknowledging their limits. The mistake to avoid is choosing all our God–images from metaphors of one gender. Masculine images of God (e.g., bridegroom of Israel, warrior, king, father) should always be balanced with feminine images. Here are some images of Yahweh which correlate with woman's experience in Israel:

- *Yahweh is like a woman giving birth.*
  Is 42:14b — Yahweh groans like a woman giving birth.
  Is 66:9 — Yahweh identifies with Zion in labor.
  Num 11:12 — Moses implies that Yahweh conceived and bore the people of Israel.

- *Yahweh is like a nursing mother.*
  Num 11:12 — Moses implies that Yahweh should be the one to nurse Israel at the breast.
  Is 49:15 — Yahweh compares her love for Israel to the love of a nursing mother for her baby.

- *Yahweh is like a mother tending a small child.*
  (It is probable that the custom at that time was for women to take charge of infants and toddlers almost exclusively.)
  Hos 11:1, 3-4 — Yahweh teaches Ephraim to walk and feeds the Israelites.
  Is 66:13 — Yahweh will comfort you like a mother.

- *Yahweh does the customary "woman's work" of putting food and water on the table.*
  (Men might bring the food into the house, but the job of transforming raw grain, oil, and newly slaughtered animals into something edible fell by custom to the women. Numerous passages in the Hebrew Scriptures mention this in passing. Many others speak of women and girls fetching water. In the following passages, Yahweh usually provides an edible meal, not raw foodstuffs. The difference is not so apparent to us, in our modern fast-food culture, but it was quite significant to the ancient Israelites, who appreciated the value of women's labor which transformed raw foodstuffs into a meal on the table.)
  Ex 16:11-16 — Yahweh provides meat and bread.
  Num 11:31-32 — Yahweh sends quail in the wilderness.
  Dt 32:13-14 — Yahweh feeds the people honey, oil, butter, milk, wheat, wine.

Ps 36:9 — Yahweh makes a feast.

Ps 81:11-17 — Yahweh fills hungry mouths with wheat and honey.

Ex 17:1-6; Num 20:2-11 — Yahweh provides water from the rock.

Neh 9:15 — Yahweh gave bread from heaven and water from the rock.

- *Yahweh is like a seamstress.*

  Neh 9:21 — Yahweh kept the people clothed in the desert.

  Gen 3:21 — Yahweh makes clothing for Adam and Eve.

- *Yahweh is like a midwife.*

  Ps 22:9-11 — Yahweh delivered me to my mother.

With these biblical images as precedent, it is appropriate to devise other feminine metaphors when speaking of God. Expressions like "the God of your fathers" and "the God of Abraham" carry an androcentric sense even though they do not make God masculine. Therefore it is best to balance them with expressions like "the God of Abraham and Sarah," "the God who spoke through the prophets and prophetesses of Israel."

TAKE ADVANTAGE OF THE WEALTH AND RANGE OF THE BIBLICAL METAPHORS WHICH DESCRIBE GOD. BALANCE MASCULINE IMAGES WITH FEMININE ONES.

4. **"Bridegroom of Israel."** The nuptial imagery found in the prophetic traditions of the Northern Kingdom must be explained in its historical and sociological context. There are two strands of this imagery: Israel as the adulterous bride of Yahweh, and Israel as prostitute. In the New Testament, Paul develops the former theme when he calls the Church the bride of Christ.

Marriage in the ancient Near East, was a relationship between two parties of unequal status and strength. Both marriage and the suzerain relationship, as they existed in the society of that day, became metaphors for the covenant between Yahweh and Israel. It is incorrect to imply that because the marriage relationship in the past served as a metaphor for the relationship between God and God's people, that marriage today must still make one partner subservient to the other.

In the region of Samaria, the Canaanite myths with their

fertility themes continued to influence Yahwistic worship long after the people of Israel had settled into the land of Canaan. This influence left its mark on the literary tradition which stems from the prophetic circles of the Northern Kingdom — especially the books of Hosea, Jeremiah, and Ezekiel.

In Canaan, the god and goddess had to be "reminded" of their duty to make crops grow every spring. The reminder took the form of ritual sex acts with temple personnel, which supposedly induced the gods to imitate this behavior. Such a practice was abhorrent to orthodox Yahwists — not because it involved sex in worship, but because it manipulated divinity. Israel's theology, developing in dialogue with heterodox cultural elements, depicted as Yahweh's spouse not another deity, but rather the lowly people of Israel. This new, Yahwistic rendering of the divine nuptial theme emphasized the supreme power and adequacy of Israel's God, and the utter dependence of Israel. Following the metaphor, Israel's infidelities to Yahweh both in worship and in political relations were termed adultery. The concept of adultery implies that the marital contract continues even though one partner has violated it.

In another metaphor, Israel is not just an adulterous wife but a prostitute. Israelites in Samaria regarded the temple personnel involved in the Canaanite fertility cults as prostitutes, and hated the idea that they forced the deity to act. Prostitution was associated with idolatry, and the Hebrew verb that means "to play the harlot" often is used to describe apostasy.

The meaning behind these metaphors does not come across without an explanation that marriage, adultery, and prostitution connote for us today something other than what they connote in the northern prophetic tradition and in the passages of Paul which stem from that tradition. In treating these themes, stress Yahweh's devotion, fidelity, forgiveness, and passion, rather than the negative portrayal of Israel as a wicked woman.

> TO BE UNDERSTOOD CORRECTLY, NUPTIAL IMAGERY FROM THE HEBREW SCRIPTURES AND PAUL ALWAYS NEEDS TO BE SET IN ITS HISTORICAL SOCIOPOLITICAL, AND RELIGIOUS CONTEXT. DO NOT EXTRAPOLATE BEYOND THE SCRIPTURAL SAYINGS ABOUT MARRIAGE AND COVENANT AND DO NOT APPLY THEM TO MARRIAGE TODAY.

Creation

5. **"God Created Them Male and Female."** The human person is the image of God — not as a self-sufficient individual but because he or she needs other people and is destined to find completion in other people. The poetry of Gen 1:27 suggests that the image of God is precisely the relatedness of humankind in its diversity. This text tells what it means to be a human being: to be human is to be godlike, to be sexually differentiated, and to be capable of prolonging creation itself. The dignity of a human being arises from this. Without woman, man would not be the image of God; man would not be godly or sexually differentiated or capable of prolonging creation. Without man, woman would not be the image of God either. God deliberated before making us this way, according to Gen 1:26, so our creation is according to God's plan. God blessed us, and saw that we were very good as God had made us.

> SHOW THAT THE DIGNITY OF HUMAN BEINGS ARISES FROM THEIR CREATION IN THE IMAGE OF GOD. THE IMAGE OF GOD IS MALE AND FEMALE.

6. **Equality of the Sexes.** Both accounts of the origin of sexual differentiation in Genesis make the point that God originally intended man and woman to be equals. In Gen 1:27, both sexes are created in a single act of the divine will. In

Gen 2:21–23, "bone of my bones" is a poetic phrase which affirms the relationship which would much later be described in the Aristotelian–Thomistic category "consubstantiality." In other words, Adam is overjoyed because he has found one like himself. He utters his first words and becomes aware of his masculine identity when he confronts the woman, whom God created without any help from the man.

The Priestly and Yahwist authors used these stories to discuss what Greek philosophers called nature or essence. The creation accounts are unique in the Hebrew Bible, in that they are the only deliberate theological pronouncement on the nature of human beings and the status of the sexes. When biblical texts later depict inequality between the sexes, they are describing the fallen condition of the race brought about by sin; these later texts do not approve the state of affairs they reflect (see #30).

THE EQUALITY OF THE SEXES IS TO BE PRESENTED AS A CLEAR MESSAGE OF THE CREATION ACCOUNTS. THESE ACCOUNTS ARE INSPIRED STATEMENTS OF GOD'S INTENT CONCERNING THE SEXES.

7. **Interdependence of the Sexes.** The interdependence of the sexes, with all of its consequences, is of divine origin and is good. If there is to be *man*, there must be women along with men. No human institution, aspiration, or reality is fully human as God would have it be if it involves only one sex to the exclusion of the other. To truncate humanity along the lines of sex is to throw away the potential for creativity which the Creator has given us. In historical accounts of achievements of the human race, the contributions of one sex are often hidden and forgotten. They should be brought to light and examined. If a human reality of any sort is portrayed as involving mostly men, either the portrayal is inaccurate or the reality is not so fully human as it could be.

IN DESCRIBING ANY HUMAN ACCOMPLISHMENT, REMEMBER TO MENTION THE CONTRIBUTIONS OF PEOPLE OF BOTH SEXES.

8. **Mutuality of the Sexes.** Women and men, who were created equal and interdependent, work out their identities and roles historically in mutual cooperation. Do not portray any group of people as having their identity defined unilaterally according to the requirements of any other group of people. That is known as *complementarity*, a word with pejorative overtones for many women.

Human beings are able to understand more than they can individually experience. Both sexes can in some way share the full range of human experiences. What one does not experience first-hand, one knows through imagination by empathically identifying with another. The woman who bears a child knows best what motherhood means, but her male and female friends do somehow share in that knowledge. Because of this human capacity for understanding, even non-parents can grasp what it means to call God "Father." Moreover, feminine imagery for Yahweh will be intelligible to anyone who understands what it is to be human. The ability to take another's viewpoint is an essential talent for making community and communication possible.

The male viewpoint that controls Scripture and Church history impoverishes theology by depriving it of the wealth of understanding available in women's experiences and even in the feminine dimension (anima) of every man. Failing to take the concerns, priorities, and experiences of others into account results in a narrow point of view that blinds one to important and interesting realities.

DO NOT TAKE THE MALE POINT OF VIEW ALL THE TIME, ESPECIALLY WHERE THE ROLES OF WOMEN ARE CONCERNED. LOOK AT THINGS FROM A VARIETY OF PERSPECTIVES.

Jesus Christ

9. **"Son of God."** This is an ancient christological title expressing the relationship of Jesus to God. It is appropriate for Jesus because he is male, but the pre-existent Logos, the second Person of the Blessed Trinity, is neither male nor female. Christians today should not be called simply "sons of God," even in hymns. Each of us is invited to be either a son or a daughter of God. By sanctifying grace, the Logos is present in women, making them daughters of God in imitation of Jesus' own sonship. It is wrong to give the impression that men can participate in Jesus' relationship with God more fully than women can.

> WHEN SPEAKING OF A COMMUNITY OF MEN AND WOMEN, ALWAYS SAY "SONS AND DAUGHTERS OF GOD."

10. **Jesus' Encounters with Women.** The gospel stories of the women in Jesus' ministry are an important source for catechesis toward justice for the sexes. Jesus seeks out women, among other "second-class citizens," to show that the reign of God is meant for them. Underline the innovative character of Jesus' treatment of women by contrasting it with prevailing customs in Palestine known from the New Testament and other sources. Jesus always sees the human and the potential for good in social outcasts and sinners. Jesus welcomes women disciples, who accompany him and the male disciples on trips. The gospel message is incomplete without the stories of these women:

- The woman taken in adultery, Jn 7:53–8:11.
- The woman with a bad name who washed Jesus' feet, Lk 7:36–50.
- The woman at the well, Jn 4:1–42. (This story can be read as an interpretation of the nuptial imagery of the northern prophetic tradition. Jesus' approach to the Samaritans — through a woman — represents the final happy reconciliation of Yahweh's marriage with these people; they "begged him to stay with them.")
- The women involved in the three instances where Jesus raises people from the dead: Jairus' daughter, Mt 9:18–19, 23–26; Mk 5:21–24, 35–43; Lk 8:40–42, 49–56; The widow of Nain's son, Lk 7:11–17; Mary and Martha's brother Lazarus, Jn 11:1–46.
- The women who are the first witnesses to the Resurrection, Mt 28:1–10; Mk 16:1–11; Lk 24:1–11; Jn 20:1–2, 11–18.
- The women whom Jesus taught and whom he counted as friends, like Mary and Martha in Lk 10:38–42, and Mary Magdalene, as well as the anonymous women in the crowds that listened to him.
- The women whom Jesus healed, like the woman with the hemorrhage, Mt 9:20–22; Mk 5:25–34; Lk 8:43–48. (Notice that Jesus calls attention to his disregard for the taboo against menstruous women.)
- The women who preached with Jesus and helped him in his work, Lk 8:1–3.

There were many women in Jesus' life. Some were weak and some were sinners, but among them also were women of courage, women of means, women of intelligence, and women who shared Jesus' ministry of proclamation.

11. **Jesus' Teachings Regarding Women.** From the way Jesus relates to women, we discern that he recognizes their full human dignity and equality with men. The word of a woman, for Jesus, is worthy to become a word of God. Jesus teaches women the word of God, and sends them to spread the word to others. (The Samaritan woman, Mary Magdalene, Johanna, and Susanna have this task.) The word of a woman is worthy witness to the Resurrection, although Jewish law did not admit the testimony of women. For Jesus, the bodies of women are not unclean; they are destined to rise from the dead. It is the words of men and women which can make them unclean (Mt 15:10-20; Mk 7:14-23); menstruation and the violation of cooking rubrics no longer count as defilement. Jesus' statement on the indissolubility of marriage was spoken in defense of women in his day, when husbands could divorce their wives and leave them destitute with little cause (Mt 19:3-10; Mk 10:2-12; Lk 16:18). In addition, Jesus often tells parables about women, and uses experiences familiar to them to make a point. Clearly, Jesus proclaims the reign of God to women and men alike. The gospel is good news for both.

EXPLAIN THE INNOVATIONS OF JESUS REGARDING
WOMEN, ESPECIALLY AS THESE RELATE TO THE PROCLA
MATION OF GOD'S WORD.

12. **Jesus and the Feminine Yahweh Imagery.** As a student of the Hebrew Scriptures, Jesus learned about his Father from the histories, the law, the prophetic oracles, the poetry, and the prayers that are the literary heritage of his people. Many of the metaphors describing Yahweh in that literature are feminine (see #3). While Jesus addressed God as "Father," it is clear that the feminine imagery spoke to his human imagination.

The gospels link the figure of Jesus to the image of Yahweh as homemaker: the one who puts food and drink on the table. We see Jesus feeding the multitudes as Yahweh fed the people in the desert (Mk 6:30-44, 8:1-10; Lk 9:12-17; Jn 6:1-15). Not only does the Jesus of the gospels wish to provide nourishment; he wants to *be* nourishment. He announces that he is the bread of life (Jn 6:34–51). He is living water (Jn 4:10–16; 7:37–38). The resonance between the eucharistic symbolism of the gospels and the feminine Yahweh imagery of the Hebrew Scriptures is quite striking and can be effectively developed in eucharistic catechesis (see #43).

Knowledge of the customs of the times also helps in understanding the import of the prophetic gestures of Jesus. The Talmud lists three affectionate personal services which a wife was expected to do for her husband, even when there were servants in the home. She was to pour her husband's wine, make his bed, and wash his face, hands, and feet (Ketubot 61a, and Rashi *ad locum*). This fact explains Peter's consternation when Jesus tries to wash his feet at the Last Supper (Jn 13:3–6). It is not that Jesus is acting like a slave; Jesus is performing the affectionate gesture of a wife! Peter clearly understands this, for upon hearing Jesus' ultimatum, he offers his head and his hands along with his feet, according to the custom.

> EXPLAIN THE FEMININE DIMENSIONS AND RESONANCES
> OF THE SYMBOLS AND GESTURES JESUS USED; SHOW
> THEIR CONNECTION TO THE FEMININE YAHWEH IMAGES
> OF THE HEBREW SCRIPTURES.

13. **Imitating Christ.** There is only one "stereotype" for the Christian: Jesus Christ is our model and paradigm. Men and women alike are called to pattern their lives after his and to imitate his virtues. Paul speaks of Christ as the new clothing, the new self which we put on at baptism (Col 3:9–10; Gal 3:27). The christic model overrides all other stereotypical role expectations for men and women. Cultural patterns for male behavior or female behavior are idolatrous if they are not made compatible with the pattern we see in Jesus. Both women and men aspire to become "other Christs" at the savior's invitation. Moreover, Christians see Christ in their brothers and sisters, without distinguishing sex. Both sexes are called to follow Christ.

> PRESENT THE IMITATION OF CHRIST AS AN EQUALLY
> ATTRACTIVE AND FEASIBLE GOAL FOR GIRLS AND BOYS.
> SHOW HOW ALL MEN AND WOMEN ARE CALLED TO BE
> CHRIST-LIKE.

14. **Virtues of Jesus.** All Christian virtues find their superlative expression in the figure of the savior. The best Christian piety sees Jesus as a fully mature and integrated human being who balances "hard" qualities (justice, fortitude, faith, wisdom, courage, zeal) with "soft" qualities (prudence, temperance, hope, charity, piety, patience, continence, meekness). All of these qualities are strengths or virtues. Jesus receives his strength from God, and shows it in different ways: sometimes in aggressive preaching or original gestures, other times in patient suffering or obedience to authority. Jesus understands his leadership to be service. It is important to portray Jesus' struggles with temptation and fear, in which he always turns to God in an attitude of obedience and receptivity. Because of Jesus' obedience, God has made him lord. Through obedience to God, Jesus was able to overcome the limits of his own male role in ancient Palestine, reaching out to women in socially frowned-upon ways and even employing feminine imagery in the symbols of unity he devised (see #43). Jesus developed virtues as he grew and matured. Like us in everything except sin, Jesus learned to practice the virtues through interactions with the women and men in his life. He learned to love the women and men whom God had given him as friends, and even enemies.

THE FIGURE OF JESUS SERVES AS AN EXAMPLE FOR CATECHESIS IN EVERY VIRTUE. DO NOT DIVIDE THE VIRTUES BETWEEN THE SEXES BY IMPLYING THAT CERTAIN ONES ARE MASCULINE OR FEMININE.

15. **Jesus' Call to Conversion.** Jesus makes it clear that the reign of God is coming upon men and women alike (Mt 24:37-41; Lk 17:34-36). The reign of God demands a radical change of heart and a turning away from old attitudes. We see in the gospels that it brings surprises and disappointments. People expected Jesus to become a king, a political messiah, a revolutionary, but Jesus resisted those role expectations and waited until God's own plan became apparent. The expectations of the world no longer need control the life-decisions of Christians. We follow Jesus in the reign of God. Rigidly defined sex roles are among the comfortable furnishings of this world which the coming of the reign of God shatters. The conversion of heart which Jesus demands is radical obedience to the will of God. Nothing can be taken for granted in the new reign. Men and women are freed from sex stereotypes for the sake of the reign of God.

> SHOW THAT JESUS' CALL TO FOLLOW HIM MEANS A RADICAL CONVERSION OF HEART AWAY FROM THE WORLD'S EXPECTATIONS, INCLUDING EXPECTATIONS BASED ON THE ASSIGNMENT OF ROLES IN SOCIETY BY SEX.

16. "The Kingdom of God." This phrase stands for the eschatological reality which Jesus' ministry announced and began. The English word *kingdom* translates the Greek *basileia* but adds an unfortunate sexist meaning to it and gives it a spatial and monarchical connotation. The phrase "reign of God," which is used in *The New American Bible* and in the *Lectionary*, is a better translation. Since the term *kingdom* is still found in older texts and heard in common speech and the Lord's Prayer, catechists should occasionally remind students that the coming age we anticipate is neither monarchical nor sexist.

There is a similar problem with the word *lord,* which translates the Hebrew *adonai* and the Greek *kyrios.* The word is customarily used both to address and to refer to each Person of the Trinity, although insofar as it implies masculine identity it is really appropriate only for Jesus Christ, "Our Lord." As there seems to be no alternative in English, God may be called "the Lord" if it is also explained that God is not male. *The New American Bible* uses "LORD" to take the place of the proper name Yahweh. In catechetical materials it is preferable to use Yahweh.

> USE "REIGN OF GOD" INSTEAD OF "KINGDOM OF GOD."
> PREFER THE PROPER NAME YAHWEH TO THE TITLE LORD.

17. Christ Figures. Jesus is a man, but the transhistorical reality of the Risen Christ transcends the masculinity of the man Jesus. The body of Christ, which is the Church, has no gender because it is an eschatological reality. There is no gender in the Eucharist. There is no gender in the Logos who is the Alpha of creation or in the Christ who is the Omega Point of humankind's aspirations. Yet this Christ is personal. To understand the reality of the Christ, it is necessary to get beyond the maleness of Jesus — as Jesus himself was able to do (see #11, 43). In our own risen bodies, our male or female sexuality will be subsumed into identity with Christ, as Paul tells us (Gal 3:28) — even if those bodies retain our sexuality along with the other components of identity that make us who we are.

Understanding of the Christ is hindered when too much emphasis is given to male images of Christ (like bridegroom of the Church), or when images like the Sacred Heart, the Good Shepherd, the Judge, or the Lamb of God receive a masculine interpretation. Images and figures of Christ must be presented in a way that lets them attract both men and women to Christ. Both sexes can identify with Christ the healer, Christ the victor, Christ the sacrificial victim, even Christ the high priest. Find other ways in which the New Testament understands Christ, other images which Jesus uses to describe himself. For example, in Mt 23:37 and Lk 13:34 Jesus says he would have liked to gather Jerusalem like a mother hen. Christ figures, both male and female, can be discovered in modern literature, too. Use these to help adolescents and adults explore the meaning of Christ.

> USE CHRIST FIGURES OF BOTH SEXES, FROM THE NEW TESTAMENT AND FROM MODERN LITERATURE, TO EX PLORE THE MEANING OF THE CHRIST.

The Holy Spirit

18. **The Spirit is Given to All.** The Spirit of Jesus is poured out abundantly on everyone in the Church at Pentecost. The Spirit enables Christians to understand their vocation and empowers the Church to proclaim the good news and carry on the ministry of Jesus. Women and men were praying together when the Spirit came at Pentecost. Accounts of Pentecost sould mention this fact, and artwork should show it clearly. The Spirit directed women and men in the ministries they performed in the early Church, and continues to direct our ministries today.

> SHOW THAT THE SPIRIT CAME EQUALLY TO MEN AND WOMEN AT PENTECOST AND DIRECTED THEIR MINISTRIES IN THE EARLY CHURCH.

19. **The Spirit of Wisdom.** The Holy Spirit is neither male nor female, but tradition has sometimes associated feminine imagery with the Spirit. The "mighty wind" of Gen 1:2 is said in some translations to hover or brood over the water; the image is that of a mother bird tending her nest. Numerous passages in the Hebrew Scriptures (e.g., Ps 36:8) speak of the shadow of the wings of God as a place of shelter. The Book of Proverbs personifies holy wisdom as a hostess

(9:1–6) and as a prophetess (1:20–33; 8:1–36). Although wisdom in Proverbs is a created thing (8:22) and the advice the book gives is more worldly than religious, the wisdom passages have been applied to the Holy Spirit. Elsewhere in the Wisdom literature, holy wisdom is quasi–divine and clearly feminine.

Early writers in the Eastern Church spoke of the Spirit of God in the feminine gender. In addition, the Sequence in the liturgy of Pentecost is a rich source of non–masculine images describing the "Creator Spirit."

TAKE ADVANTAGE OF FEMININE IMAGERY, SUCH AS THE DEPICTION OF WISDOM IN THE HEBREW SCRIPTURES WHEN DISCUSSING THE HOLY SPIRIT.

20. **Gifts and Fruits of the Spirit.** Christian tradition designates certain qualities as *gifts* which the Spirit brings: wisdom, understanding, counsel, fortitude, knowledge, piety, fear of the Lord. Certain other qualities are called *fruits* and are taken as evidence that the Spirit has been at work in a person: charity, joy, peace, patience, benignity, goodness, long–suffering, mildness, faith, modesty, continency, chastity. Since the Spirit is poured out equally on men and women, one should look for the gifts and fruits in equal measure in both sexes. With the passing of time, however, there has been a tendency to identify the *gifts* with hierarchical ordained ministry and therefore with men, and to identify the *fruits* with charismatic nonordained ministries and the women who perform them. This overspecialization is dysfunctional for the reign of God. In its extreme form, it is caricature that must be deliberately counteracted. Men in ordained ministries should be depicted as patient, long–suffering, etc. — as well as wise, pious, etc. Women in the charismatic ministries of caring and service should be depicted as knowledgeable, strong–willed, etc. — as well as charitable, mild, etc. Encourage both sexes to develop the gifts which the Spirit gives and to manifest the fruits of the Spirit's work.

AVOID THE STEREOTYPE OF ASSIGNING THE "GIFTS OF THE SPIRIT" TO MEN AND THE "FRUITS OF THE SPIRIT" TO WOMEN.

The Church

21. **The Church is not She.** In English the neuter pronoun is proper with the noun *church*. Even though translations of Vatican documents sometimes call the Church *she*, the usage is incorrect. Scripture describes the Church in feminine metaphors, but these by no means ascribe a feminine identity to the Church. Paul calls the Church our mother when he compares it to Abraham's freeborn wife whose child carried the Promise (Gal 4:26). The woman in the Book of Revelation is identified with the Church (Rev 12:17). Both of these passages need careful exegesis.

The image of *mother Church* is overworked. Look for alternatives in Scripture, in the documents of Vatican II, and in the theological tradition. Use a range of metaphors to explain the complex reality of the Church.

> THE CHURCH IS NOT A FEMININE ENTITY; REFER TO IT
> AS "IT." COMPLEMENT THE METAPHOR OF MOTHER
> CHURCH WITH OTHER IMAGES OF THE CHURCH.

22. **"Bride of Christ."** The image of the Church as Christ's bride should be explained as a development of the nuptial imagery of the northern prophetic tradition, which pictured Israel as the bride of Yahweh (see #4). Paul uses this image to make the theological point that the Church is the "new

Israel," so to speak, that is, the people of God. The metaphor is hardly intelligible apart from the literary tradition from which it comes. Paul compares the relationship of husband and wife with the relationship of Christ and the Church (Eph 5:21–33). The Book of Revelation, using vivid apocalyptic and mythological language, calls the Church the bride of the Lamb (19:7–10; 21:2, 9–10; 22:17). This bride is the New Jerusalem — *not* the woman who was identified in 12:17 as mother Church. The New Testament writers use a variety of images to develop their accounts of the mysterious reality that is the Church. It is advisable to do likewise in catechetical materials. The Pauline theme of the Church as "body of Christ" complements the bridal theme nicely. Take care not to stretch any ecclesial metaphor beyond its legitimate meaning.

EXPLAIN THAT THE IMAGE "BRIDE OF CHRIST" HAS ITS
ROOTS IN THE NUPTIAL METAPHORS OF THE NORTHERN
PROPHETIC TRADITION.

23. **Priesthood.** It is a fact of life in the Roman Catholic Church at this time that all priests are men. Help students understand this by explaining the historical and social conditions that gave rise to it as well as the pastoral considerations that support it. Avoid giving the impression that "girls are not good enough" to become priests. Emphasize the importance of the universal call to priesthood received in baptism. Historically, the ministries arose in response to needs in the Church. The hierarchical ordained ministry is a special call within the larger ecclesial context. It exists to coordinate and serve the other ministries. As presider at the Eucharistic celebration, the priest administers the sacrament of unity which nourishes the members of the Church so that they can perform their own ministries in union with Christ and one another.

Priestly celibacy needs careful treatment because there is a long history of misogynism associated with it that must be counteracted. Do not give the impression that women distract priests or divert them from God. Priests need women as coworkers, advisers, and friends. Depict priests with a normal range of social relationships, interacting with lay men and women, religious, and other priests.

PRESENT THE HISTORICAL AND PASTORAL REASONS FOR
THE PRESENT LIMITATION OF PRIESTHOOD TO MEN. DO
NOT IMPLY THAT WOMEN ARE NOT GOOD ENOUGH,
INTELLIGENT ENOUGH, OR STRONG ENOUGH TO BE
PRIESTS. COUNTERACT THE IDEA THAT WOMEN EN-
DANGER THE VOCATIONS OF MALE PRIESTS.

24. **Liturgical Roles.** In art and in texts, portray women filling all the liturgical roles which they now perform in the United States: lectors, cantors, ministers of the Eucharist, musicians, dancers, and ushers. Show that women plan liturgies along with celebrants and other participants. Women teach liturgical theology and homiletics to priests, seminarians, and other students. Women also design and build churches and church furnishings. They make statues and other artwork for churches. They create vestments, altar linens, banners, chalices, and the other implements needed at Mass. They make wine and bake bread for the altar. They write hymns and prayers, and compose music for worship. They work on the translation and adaptation of rites. Women catechists help the people prepare for liturgical celebration and reflect upon it afterwards. Congregations of women religious sing or recite the Liturgy of the Hours every day; this is the prayer of the Church, even though no one in Orders is present.

Encourage open dialogue on the questions of altar girls and women's ordination; help students to see the pastoral and theological issues involved.

DEPICT WOMEN IN A VARIETY OF LITURGICAL ROLES.
DISCUSS THE WAYS IN WHICH WOMEN CONTRIBUTE
TO THE CELEBRATION OF THE LITURGY.

25. **Profile of the Priest.** Portray the priest as a well-rounded human being with strengths and weaknesses like everyone else. Catechetical materials should show that the diocesan priest participates in all the affairs of his parish, diocese, or institution. He is interested in activities involving men and women, separately or together. He roots for the girls' softball team as well as for the boys' soccer team. He attends the sodality luncheon, the Knights of Columbus communion breakfast, and the youth group disco. The priest is often an adviser or helper, but often he seeks help for himself or for another. Laywomen, laymen, religious of both sexes, and other priests enter his life in a variety of professional and social roles. He has parents, brothers and sisters, nieces and nephews. Priests who have chosen the monastic life might not encounter women on a daily basis; most others do. Avoid stereotyping the priest as a macho sports coach, an other-worldly dreamer, or a super-teacher called into the classroom to settle the hard questions. Avoid clericalism in describing the administration of parish or diocese and in depicting the priest's social and professional relationships. The priest aims to integrate the aesthetic side of his personality with the athletic, the gregarious with the contemplative, the scholarly with the practical. He develops his personal talents for the service of God's people.

PORTRAY PRIESTS PARTICIPATING IN ACTIVITIES IN-VOLVING MEN AND WOMEN, GIRLS AND BOYS. AVOID CLERICAL STEREOTYPES; DEPICT PRIESTS' PROFES-SIONAL, SOCIAL AND FAMILY RELATIONSHIPS WITH PEOPLE OF BOTH SEXES.

26. **Women Ministering Today.** Women fulfill a great number of ministries in the United States today. Not every job is a ministry, of course. It might be said that a ministry entails three things: service to the people of God, an intention on the minister's part to work on behalf of the Church for the Church, and some sort of commission from the Christian community. Baptism is the basic validation which the Church gives for many of the ministries which Christians perform. However, the more deliberate and ecclesially articulated the ministry, the greater the need for the Christian community to recognize and support it. The community can discern when the work undertaken by a baptized person becomes an ecclesial ministry, and should support the ministries which it recognizes.

It is important to depict the value and the variety of the work women do in the Church today. Make these jobs appear attractive and worthwhile as career choices for young women and girls. Some of the jobs need definition to show their connection with the mission of the Church. For example, a physician can understand her job as a lucrative profession, or as a way to follow Christ in the ministry of healing.

Programs of adult catechesis and parish outreach should aim to introduce women and men involved in these occupations to ways in which they can make them expressions of the Church's mission, and therefore ministries. The local Church should express its support for newly recognized ministries as well as for conventional ones. Women religious have pioneered in taking unusual jobs and defining them as ministries. Take note of this contribution as well as the more traditional ministries which women religious have performed. Also depict the contributions of lay women in conventional and newly discovered ministries. Portray women ministering to both women and men, girls and boys.

DEPICT THE VARIETY AND THE VALUE OF MINISTRIES WHICH WOMEN PERFORM IN THE UNITED STATES TODAY. INVITE COMMUNITIES TO NOTICE WORKS WHICH DESERVE THEIR RECOGNITION AND SUPPORT AS ECCLESIAL MINISTRIES.

27. Third-World Ministries.
Women take on extraordinary ministerial duties in places where there are too few ordained priests. Women administer parishes in Appalachia and in American Indian territories. In Brazil and Chile, women do the work of pastors. Present these situations to show the variety that exists in the universal Church. The circumstances in mission lands, post–Christian Western Europe, China and the Soviet Union intensify the Church's need for more ministers to evangelize the people of these lands and to care for their pastoral needs. Some areas of the United States and some ethnic groups within this nation also need concentrated evangelization and pastoral care. Show what women are accomplishing in such situations. The catechetical goal is to invite a generous response from young women and men to the needs of the third–world churches, and to engender support for third–world ministers among the Christians of the United States.

SHOW THE EXTRAORDINARY MINISTRIES WHICH WOMEN PERFORM IN CHURCHES WHICH HAVE EXTRAORDINARY NEEDS.

28. Biblical Women. Women played an essential role in salvation history and the fulfillment of God's promise to Israel. At the very least, God's covenant with Abraham depended on Sarah, for both together had those descendants numerous as the stars. Matthew's genealogy of Jesus makes a point of naming some of his female ancestors among the people through whom the promise was transmitted — a theologically significant departure from the usual listing of forefathers only. The key figures at the very beginning of the Exodus story are all women: Moses' mother, the Hebrew midwives, Miriam, Pharoah's daughter and her maids (Ex 2:2–10).

In addition to the women directly involved in the fulfillment of God's promise, the Bible preserves the stories of other women who excelled in their service to the nation, their intelligence, their political power, or their attunement to the word of Yahweh.

Deborah, Huldah, and Noadiah are three prophetesses. Noadiah is mentioned in passing in Neh 6:14. Huldah founded the biblical canon when she certified the newly discovered *Book of the Law* (2 Kgs 22:11–20; 2 Chr 34:22–28). Deborah was a judge of civil disputes who also marched to battle at the head of 10,000 men (Jg 4:4–16).

Jael assassinated Sisera (the Canaanite general whose army Deborah's defeated, Jg 4:17–21) by putting him to sleep with warm milk and driving a tent peg into his head. Athaliah, queen of the kingdom of Judah, eliminated the royal family and ruled for six years (2 Kgs 11:1–3; 2 Chr 22:10–12).

The Queen of Sheba was Solomon's match in wit and wealth; she freely debated with him (1 Kgs 10:1–13). Bathsheba, as queen mother during Solomon's reign, was recognized as an effective lobbyist with the king; when she went to court to speak with Solomon she sat at his right hand (1 Kgs 2:12–25).

Miriam is named along with her brothers as a leader whom Yahweh sent to Israel (Mic 6:4). Yahweh summons Miriam, Aaron, and Moses into the Tent of Meeting to settle a dispute among them (Num 12:1–10), although so close an encounter with the cult has curious consequences for Miriam. Abigail, a woman of intelligence and beauty, stages a demonstration of hospitality that convinces David, just in a nick of time, not to slaughter her household because of her husband's stupidity (1 Sam 25:2-35).

In addition, the stories of Ruth, Judith, and Esther are well known. The Book of Ruth is especially useful to emphasize the role of women in salvation history, while the books of Esther and Judith illustrate women's service to the nation.

Some of the more unsavory characters of the Hebrew Bible also are women. In telling their stories, explain the historical and sociopolitical situation. When the Bible attributes wiley, sneaky, or devious tactics to women, point out that a class of people who lack legitimate access to power sometimes find other ways to operate. Moreover, political and social ethics in ancient Israel were quite different from our own, as the stories of Jacob and other Israelite men attest.

The Bible often refers to a tribe or nation by the name of its patriarch (e.g., Ephraim, Judah, Israel), and therefore in our translations the masculine singular pronoun is used to stand for the whole people. Point out that this is just an archaic figure of speech. The people of Israel was always composed of both men and women. Catechetical materials should speak of the men *and* women of Israel and of the primitive Church.

THE CHOSEN PEOPLE ARE OF BOTH SEXES. MAKE A POINT OF REFERRING TO THE "MEN AND WOMEN" OF THE PROMISE. TELL THE STORIES OF THE WOMEN IN THE HEBREW BIBLE, PRESENTING THEIR SOCIAL, POLITICAL, AND HISTORICAL CONTEXTS.

29. Words of Biblical Women. The oracles, canticles, and conversations of the women in the Bible provide an insight into how they spoke to God and to other women and men. While these discourses most likely were recorded by men and may be literary devices, they do portray women positively as autonomous, articulate, thoughtful persons. Some of the discourses which deserve catechetical attention are the following:

- The Song of Deborah and Barak, Jg 5:1-31;
- The Song of Hannah, 1 Sam 2:1-10;
- Ruth's conversation with Naomi, Ru 1:8-22;
- Mary's conversation with the angel, Lk 1:26-38;

- Mary's "Magnificat," Lk 1:46–55;
- Mary's request of Jesus at Cana, Jn 2:1–5;
- The Samaritan's conversation with Jesus at Jacob's well, Jn 4:7–30;
- The Syrophoenician's witty response which convinced Jesus to heal her child, Mt 15:21–28, Mk 8:24-30.

THE BIBLE GIVES WOMEN SPEAKING PARTS. THEIR WORDS SHOW THEM TO BE INTELLIGENT, AUTONOMOUS PERSONS. MAKE USE OF THESE WORDS TO ACHIEVE POSITIVE IMAGES OF WOMEN IN CATECHETICAL MATERIALS.

30. **Biblical Attitudes Toward Women.** Biblical texts express contradictory attitudes about women. Several important principles govern interpretation in this area. First, descriptive texts are to be distinguished from normative texts, and provisional norms from unconditional norms. The Bible presents very few unconditionally normative texts concerning the status of women, that is, theological statements about the nature of women. These include the creation accounts (Gen 1:27 and 2:21–23), and Gal 3:23–28. Many of the laws of the Hebrew Scriptures, as well as the pastoral rulings recorded in the Pauline corpus, are provisional norms meant to apply in specific situations. They need careful interpretation today.

The bulk of biblical texts which convey something about the status of the sexes are descriptive texts. We read between the lines of the historical, cultic, or wisdom material to discern statements about prevailing attitudes toward women. The statements are of historical interest, but are not normative. They merely describe the way women were treated in a certain time and place among people whom the Bible admits were sinful people.

The second hermeneutical principle is that later texts can interpret and refine earlier ones. The entire New Testament reinterprets the Hebrew Scriptures. Paul's thought is seen to develop from his early epistles to his later ones, so that what he says in his later writings tells us how to understand his earlier material (see #31).

The third hermeneutical principle rests on the theological

assumption that Jesus' attitude toward women is normative for the Christian. Jesus' teachings about the sexes override the attitudes expressed in the Hebrew Scripture. In Mt 19:4-6 we find that Jesus affirms the theological statements of equality made in Gen 1 and 2 (see #11).

With these principles in mind, it is important to draw attention to the Bible's negative attitudes toward women. Much of the writing adopts an exclusively male viewpoint as if the intended audience did not include women. This fact must be pointed out as an historical accident that is by no means an essential characteristic of the word of God. It shows up particularly in the law. The apodictic laws (the "thou shalt not's") are addressed to men, for the Hebrew uses a masculine singular form. Casuistic law (consisting of cases that begin with the formula "If a man . . .") also concerns itself almost entirely with men. This peculiarity has been explained in terms of the Hebrew social system. The unit of society was not the individual but the family, and a man stood for his family.

Aside from its androcentric viewpoint, the Bible is at times openly misogynistic. Again, the laws define menstruous women as unclean (Lev 15:19-30). A mother who has borne a male infant is unclean for seven days, while the mother of a baby girl is unclean for fourteen days (Lev 12.2-5). In the historical books, we find women used as a bribe in the Sodom story (Gen 19:1-10). The aged David is given a girl as a bed-warmer (1 Kgs 1:1-4). Numerous passages in the Book of Proverbs belittle women (e.g., 5:3-6, 19:13, 21:9, 19). Women are caricatured as troublesome, nagging, and treacherously persuasive.

Explain that these negative attitudes come from the cultures in which the biblical authors lived rather than from the inspiration of God. A good example of a biblical attitude that we have outgrown is the attitude toward childless marriages. The ancient people of Israel, who did not understand the biology of reproduction, thought that a "barren" woman was cursed by God. A woman could even be divorced for barrenness. Today we know that there is no moral fault involved in failure to produce children — for either husband or wife. Therefore, the earlier biblical view of childless women is a historically contingent attitude, certainly not valid today. It is important to prepare students for the negative views of women which they will find in the Bible.

On the other hand, the Bible expresses some positive attitudes toward women that are still valid for Christians. Motherhood, for example, was esteemed in ancient Israel as it is now. In the Hebrew Scriptures, motherhood was considered the highest status a woman could achieve; even Deborah the warrior–judge is praised as "a mother in Israel" (Jg 5:7). But Jesus sets other things above motherhood. For Jesus it is more blessed to hear and keep the word of God than to be a mother, even the mother of the messiah (Lk 11:27–28; cf. Mk 3:31–35).

CAREFULLY DISTINGUISH PRESCRIPTIVE FROM DESCRIPTIVE TEXTS WHEN PRESENTING BIBLICAL ATTITUDES TOWARD WOMEN. HELP STUDENTS TO DEAL WITH THE ANDROCENTRIC VIEWPOINT AND MISOGYNIST TONE OF MANY BIBLICAL PASSAGES.

31. **Paul.** Writings attributed to this apostle present us with some of the most troublesome texts concerning women. At first glance, he seems inconsistent. He proclaims freedom from the law. Then he tells women to keep quiet in the assembly because custom requires it (1 Cor 14:34). The inconsistency, apparent to us who can look at Paul's epistles all together, simply indicates that Paul's thought developed gradually and that he wrote in response to a variety of circumstances.

With Paul, context is always important — both the internal context of a given text within an epistle and within the whole body of Paul's writings, and the external circumstances that caused the given text to be written. Never cite Paul out of these two contexts; it only leads to misunderstanding. Paul's basic perspective is an eschatological one. He sees this world passing away because Christ has liberated us from it. This perspective finds expression in Paul's theology before it becomes operative in his social thinking. He realized the social implications of the new freedom in Christ only gradually.

The following texts present problems, and need careful treatment in catechetical materials and in homilies:

- 1 Cor 11:4–10, where Paul requires women to wear veils in Church;
- 1 Cor 14:35, where Paul requires women to keep silent in Church;

- Eph 5:21-33, where wives are told to submit to their husbands;
- 1 Tim 2:9-15, where women are denied permission to teach.

The two texts from 1 Cor are pastoral advice given in response to questions that apparently arose out of some dispute in the worshiping assembly at Corinth. The first text is followed immediately and softened by a reminder that both men and women come from God (1 Cor 11:11-12). The next sentence (vv. 13-15) is a rhetorical question asking whether common sense does not support Paul's ruling. Apparently Paul expects a *negative* answer, for the next verse seeks to stop the argument with a final blow: it is simply not the custom for women to pray with their hair uncovered.

In 1 Cor 14:35, Paul is again trying to settle a dispute that has been referred to him. The advice to "ask their husbands" seems curious because Paul knows he is addressing a congregation in which a good many women have no husbands (see chapter 7 of the same letter). The two texts from 1 Cor, as pastoral advice, are overshadowed theologically by Paul's description of the interdependence of the Body of Christ (1 Cor 12:12-30) and by his proclamation of the New Creation (2 Cor 5:17). In Gal 3:27-29 Paul affirms that both men and women share equally in the promise and in Christ. In Gal 5:6, he overturns circumcision, which had been a gender-related badge of participation in the Covenant. Baptism is always equal for both sexes.

The two other texts, Eph 5:21-33 and 1 Tim 2:9-15, belong to later epistles which scholars feel may have been composed by someone other than Paul. They reflect a later situation in the Church, when the urgency of Paul's eschatological perspective had faded, and should be explained in that context. We know, for example, that Paul did indeed permit women to teach. He mentions some of his women coworkers: Chloe (1 Cor 1:11), Phoebe, Prisca or Priscilla, and Mary (Rom 16:1-7).

PAUL'S THEOLOGICAL AFFIRMATION OF EQUALITY IN CHRIST OVERSHADOWS THE PASTORAL RULINGS HE GIVES FOR PARTICULAR SITUATIONS. ALWAYS SITUATE PAULINE TEXTS IN THE CONTEXT OF HIS ENTIRE THEO-LOGICAL DEVELOPMENT AND INDICATE THE SITUATION FOR WHICH THEY WERE WRITTEN.

32. **Luke.** The Gospel of Luke provides a model for catechesis addressed to both sexes. We know that among the first converts there were many women, especially from the upper classes of Hellenistic society. Luke aims to bring the gospel message home to each person in an audience composed of both sexes. He records the parables of Jesus in pairs: one makes a point especially for the men; the other makes the same point in terms calculated to reach women. For example, the parable of the man and the lost sheep (15:3-7) is followed immediately by the parable of the woman and the lost coin (15:8-10); the Good Samaritan tale is addressed to the men (10:38-42); the centurian's servant is healed (7:2-10), and then Jesus takes pity on a widow and raises her only son from the dead (7:11-17). Metaphors for the reign of God arise from both male and female occupations: there is the mustard seed, which farmers will understand, and the yeast, which homemakers will understand (13:18-21). Each sex is addressed in terms most familiar to its particular life situation, yet everyone can grasp both versions and take the message to heart.

Since the other Synoptics also make use of similar pairings, this targeting technique must have been among the earliest Christian catechetical tools.

> FOLLOWING THE TRADITION OF THE EARLIEST RE-CORDED CHRISTIAN CATECHESIS, FINE-TUNE THE MES-SAGE WITH ILLUSTRATIONS FROM THE HEARERS' DIFFER-ENT WORLDS OF EXPERIENCE.

33. **Acts.** Women made important contributions to the spread of the gospel and to the life of the early Christian community, a fact well documented in the Acts of the Apostles. In the first century, upper-class women in the Hellenistic culture of the Roman Empire, unlike their contemporaries in Palestine, were achieving some autonomy and control over property. This circumstance proved providential for the spread of the gospel, because a number of those women opened their houses and coffers to the Church — supporting it, protecting it, and leading it.

The dictum that Christianity raised the social status of women is inaccurate. A few women in the Greco-Roman world already enjoyed power and social standing, and when they received Christ, were well-prepared to help the Church grow (Acts 17:4). As the Church eroded the barriers between Jew and Greek, some interesting clashes of culture ensued. We find Paul trying to impose the traditional mores of Palestinian Jews upon the women of Corinth, who were accustomed to speak their minds in public (see #31).

As the centuries passed, the trend was for women to be silenced, veiled, and shut out of visible Church life, but in the beginning women were there when the Church needed them. The contributions of women like the following must not be neglected in catechesis.

Priscilla, who with her husband Aquila worked and traveled with Paul, opened her house for the Church to meet there, and taught the gospel; Acts 18:18, 26; cf. 1 Cor 16:19;

Lydia of Thyatira, a dealer in purple dye, who invited Paul and his party to stay at her home had her whole household baptized, Acts 16:14-15;

Tabitha or Dorcas, called a disciple, who took care of the poor in Jaffa was raised from the dead after Peter prayed for her, Acts 9:36-42.

POINT OUT THE WAYS IN WHICH THE SPIRITUAL AND MATERIAL GIFTS OF WOMEN HELPED THE CHURCH GROW. TELL THE STORIES OF THE WOMEN MENTIONED IN THE ACTS OF THE APOSTLES.

34. Women in Church History. The *whole* story of Christianity is a story of women and men *together*. A history of the Church is incomplete if it fails to tell what women were doing and saying in each period. Recount the lives of individual women who influenced the Church's development. Do not forget the millions of anonymous women and men whose lives were affected by the actions of the great and the powerful.

During every historical period, the faithful included men and women in virtually equal numbers. Do not say things like, "The men of the thirteenth century built Gothic cathedrals." If indeed it is true that those who did the heavy labor were primarily men, then tell how the construction project affected the economy and family life of the town and how the women fit into the total picture.

Women went on pilgrimages and crusades, founded monasteries, ruled nations, led reforms, and sponsored scholars and artists. Mention the literary achievements of women. Make it a point to show artwork created by women: illuminated manuscripts, embroidery, tapestry. Explore the sociological and cultural factors in the exclusion of women from the other arts.

The shameful story of ecclesiastical oppression of women must also be told. The systematic misogynism of theology had its counterparts in canon law and official Church policies toward women. Explore the reasons for this as well as the effects it had and is still having on women, on the Church, and on society. Assess the relationship between practices in the Church and practices in society at large.

> TELL THE WHOLE STORY OF THE HISTORY OF THE CHURCH. DELINEATE THE ROLES PLAYED BY WOMEN IN EVERY AGE. BE CAREFUL TO REFER TO THE "MEN AND WOMEN" IN THE CHURCH. DESCRIBE THE SYSTEMATIC DISCRIMINATION AGAINST WOMEN BY THE CHURCH.

35. **Patrology.** Christian writers of the first few centuries are known in the theological trade as "the fathers." The discipline which studies them is called patrology. While it is true that most of the authors whose works come down to us from this period are men, both of these terms are sexist and should be avoided. "Early Christian writers" is an alternative to "the fathers." Catechetical materials might mention the writings of one woman of this period, Egeria, a pilgrim whose diary gives accounts of the liturgy in Jerusalem in the early fifth century and serves as an invaluable historical source because of its careful attention to detail.

Some of the most bizarre misogynist passages in all of world literature can be found in the pages of Augustine, Jerome, Tertullian, Justin Martyr, Irenaeus, Clement of Alexandria, John Chrysostom, and Origen. Point out that their mistaken ideas influenced all subsequent theology.

> REFER TO "THE FATHERS" AS "EARLY CHRISTIAN WRITERS." EXPLAIN THAT NOT EVERYTHING THEY WROTE WAS CHRISTIAN.

36. **Evolution of the Female Religious.** Communities of women have fulfilled important and varied roles throughout the history of the Church. The convent became a sphere of independent activity for many women of great talent and sanctity. Often they worked against discouraging obstacles, some of which were imposed by male authorities who wished to circumscribe and "protect" the sisters. Point out the achievements and contributions of women's religious communities, especially in this country — for example, in the parochial schools and in health care. Tell the interesting stories of dual foundations and of double monsteries, where abbesses sometimes had authority over monks and priests. The role of the sister has evolved over the centuries, and today there are different sorts of religious life open to women. The traditions and accomplishments of religious communities of women are a heritage for everyone in the Church.

PORTRAY THE HISTORY OF RELIGIOUS LIFE AMONG WOMEN. POINT OUT THE CONTRIBUTIONS OF THE SISTERS TO THE CHURCH, ESPECIALLY THE CHURCH IN THE UNITED STATES.

37. **States of Life.** People in the Church come from a variety of backgrounds and lifestyles. Catechetical materials and programs should reflect this diversity. Among Church members are parents and non-parents, the young and the old, individuals who are married, single, divorced, separated, widowed, vowed to religious life, ordained to the service of God's people. Every Church member has the right to receive catechesis. Materials and programs should be developed for the special needs of each.

Materials must present a balanced view of Church life by showing both sexes participating in the parish and diocese. One's membership in the Church and participation in parish activities has nothing to do with marital status or sexual orientation. Portray both sexes as youth ministers, catechists, liturgists, and members of parish councils and committees. Avoid the stereotype of the old maid who devotes herself to the altar society and cleans the church, or the busy bachelor professional man who is called in as a special adviser. Show how elderly women and men take part in parish life. Mention women with special needs: housebound mothers of small children, elderly women, women with problem pregnancies, women in prisons, and so forth. Portray such parish services as day-care centers and women's self-help groups, along with the more traditional women's parish activities.

Avoid assigning more worth to one state of life than to others. Religious celibacy is a special gift which God gives the individual — but so are parenthood, marriage, and single life. Each of these has both actual and symbolic value; each can become a sign of the reign of God.

> DEVELOP CATECHETICAL PROGRAMS AND MATERIALS FOR PEOPLE IN ALL STATES OF LIFE. MATERIALS SHOULD DEPICT CHURCH MEMBERS FROM A VARIETY OF BACKGROUNDS.

The Sacraments

38. **Liturgical Texts.** Catechesis aims to lead Christians toward the fullest possible understanding of and participation in liturgy. Two kinds of liturgical texts can impede this purpose. First, Scripture passages with negative images of women sometimes come up in the Lectionary. Homilists can find suggestions for handling such passages in #4,5,6,10,11,12,28,29,30,31,32,33,43 of these guidelines. The Lectionary presents readings with positive images of women as well, which give homilists the opportunity to catechize in the spirit of these guidelines.

The second kind of troublesome liturgical text comes from the Roman Ritual and its English translation. There are several striking instances of unnecessary sexist language in the Ordinary parts of the Mass. In the Creed: "For *us men* and for our salvation he came down from heaven." In the Eucharistic Prayers: "It will be shed for you and for *all men* so that sins may be forgiven." Both homilists and catechists have to explain these two phrases in a way that will make it clear that *men* denotes both sexes. Help girls and women to hear *men* as a word that includes themselves. Point out that the word *man* in Canon IV and in the Creed translates the Latin *homo* (human being), not *vir* (male man). The explanation should go into as much historical and philological detail as the audience can understand. Show that meaning can transcend the words that express it. These words are inexact translations that may be changed in the future.

EXPLAIN THAT THE CREED AND THE WORDS OF CONSE-
CRATION MEAN TO INCLUDE WOMEN AS "MEN." HOMI-
LISTS SHOULD RELFECT ON PASSAGES FROM THE LEC-
TIONARY IN THE SPIRIT OF THESE GUIDELINES.

39. **Hymns and Responsorial Psalms.** One often encounters sexist or androcentric language in the hymns and
psalm responses used at Mass. Encourage girls and boys to
listen for these unfortunate phrases and to recognize them as
relics from the past. It is important not to let exposure to
androcentric language at liturgy spoil the catechesis toward
justice for the sexes which young people receive elsewhere.

Often catechists and youth ministers have some control over
the choice of hymns and psalms for Mass and for less formal
prayer services. Wherever possible, avoid sexist and androcentric lyrics. Hymns printed in catechetical materials should never
be sexist. If a hymn is worth salvaging, seek permission from
the copyright holder to adjust the words, for instance by
changing men to all, us, one, you, etc., or by alternating
masculine and feminine pronouns. On the positive side, look for
hymns and songs that express positive attitudes toward justice
for the sexes, in harmony with these guidelines. Publishers
seeking to present non–sexist lyrics should be encouraged.

The psalms often use androcentric language, which should be
adjusted before they are employed in prayer in a catechesial
situation. (Indeed, a few of the imprecatory psalms express such
jarring sentiments that they are not used in Christian worship
at all.) Psalms are interpreted in liturgy through use of an
antiphon, a short verse from the psalm itself or from another
source, which the people repeat between the verses of the
psalm. When preparing services of the word, take care to avoid
sexist and androcentric antiphons, particularly of the "Happy
the man . . ." variety. A good antiphon can be used to correct an
androcentric psalm.

40. **Services of the Word.** Prayer meetings, reconciliation services, and other services of the word can be
occasions for catechesis toward justice for the sexes. The power
of God's word heals the scars of sexism. Plan services around
themes like human dignity, conversion, freedom in Christ,
response to God's creative call. Teachers' manuals should make
suggestions for such services. Choose Scripture texts like those
listed in #3,6,10,12,15,28,29,31,32,33,43 of these guidelines.
Choose psalms, hymns, and popular music in the spirit of these
guidelines. Explore sacred dance and the use of gestures of
reconciliation and acceptance by both sexes. Readings from the
Hebrew Scriptures and accounts of Jesus' encounters with
women can be dramatized. Ritualize the reconciliation and
reciprocal acceptance between the sexes that characterizes our
new being–together in the reign of God.

PLAN SERVICES OF THE WORD TO AUGMENT THE CATE-
CHETICAL EFFORT TOWARD JUSTICE FOR THE SEXES.

41. **Catechesis for Baptism.** Baptism is the same for
men and women. Both are equally in Christ and
members of the Church. Baptism abolishes the distinctions
among classes of people. In Christ there is no longer male or
female (Gal 3:28). The reign of God overtakes both sexes;
salvation comes equally to both. Mention these points when the
sacrament of baptism is explained.

People who are baptized have been set free from the sin of
sexism and from the coercive stereotypes related to it. Catechesis for parents before the baptism of their child should
encourage them to shield the child from learning sexist
attitudes. Where there is an organized adult catechumenate,
catechesis toward justice for the sexes should form part of the
course of studies. (See also the discussion of original sin, #46.)

42. **Catechesis for Confirmation.** Reception of the fullness of the Spirit signifies freedom and empowerment. The confirmed person will be taking on new responsibility for herself or himself, and at the same time finding new
opportunities for personal fulfillment and commitment. Adapt
the catechesis to the age of those being confirmed, not to their
sex. Both women and men need the strengthening of the Spirit
to lead the Christian life courageously and to contribute their
talents for the good of the community. Like baptism, confirmation is the same for both sexes. Themes presented in
#18,19,20,26,27,33 of these guidelines can be developed
appropriately for confirmation catechesis.

THE SPIRIT COMES EQUALLY TO MEN AND WOMEN IN
CONFIRMATION, STRENGTHENING THEM TO FOLLOW
CHRIST AND SERVE THE COMMUNITY.

43. **Eucharistic Catechesis.** The life of Christ which we
share in the Eucharist unites us, overcoming the
divisiveness of sexist role definitions. Because we encounter
Christ and one another in the Eucharist, Christians are enabled
to see Christ in their sisters and brothers. The Eucharist can
overcome the barriers that oppress the sexes, because Jesus
Christ overcame them in his own life. Fully a man, he
transcended the boundaries of his own maleness in his deeds,
his doctrine, and his poetic logic. Jesus' ministry to women often
went beyond the pale of what was socially acceptable (see #10).
Jesus' doctrine about women proclaims that their bodies are
destined to rise, and their words are worthy to become
evangelizing words of God (see #11). Jesus' logic employs
symbols and images from both male and female experience to
express the truth of God (see #12).

While we do not today have access to the consciousness of
Jesus and cannot study him psychologically, catechetical
discourse can legitimately lead people in meditation that

imaginatively explores the personality behind the figure who meets us in the gospels. The Jesus of the gospels is the same Jesus whom we know in the sacrament of the Eucharist and in the eucharistic community. To foster love and a personal relationship with this Jesus, catechesis might well encourage reflection along the following lines.

The savior was no stranger to any human experience. He understood the men and women, girls and boys among whom he lived. As an integrated, mature human being, he shared empathically in their lives. He must have seen what it was to fall in love and marry (if it did not actually happen to him); he knew about childbirth and widowhood and old age (although these were not his very own experiences). Sometimes he wanted to express things for which there was no analogue in his own young male existence. Then, he reached into his imagination and found pictures for what he wished to say in the experiences of other people. This was no supernatural power; all poets do this. The Word Incarnate was heir to the entire range of human expression, as well as to the manifold imagery in which Yahweh was revealed in the Hebrew Scripture.

Why did Jesus choose bread and wine as the eucharistic elements? Each is one thing made from many things. They express the unification which Jesus wanted the Eucharist to accomplish. Jesus often must have seen women at work, grinding the grains of wheat or barley into flour, sifting it, kneading the dough, baking the loaves. He saw men and women crushing the grapes, straining out the juice, setting it aside to ferment, producing wine. He saw (perhaps he shared in) the cooperative labor in fields and vineyards. He enjoyed the table fellowship where the fruits of the labor were consumed. Perhaps he thought to himself, I want to be unity and joy for my people, like bread and wine.

Meditating further on the symbolic resonances of the Eucharist, catechesis can suggest that Jesus identified with the images of Yahweh he found in the Hebrew Scriptures, where he saw Yahweh depicted as a woman in labor and a nursing mother (see #3). These images express how Jesus feels toward his people, just as they show how Yahweh feels toward Israel. The eucharistic utterances of the Johannine Jesus propose a double riddle. What kind of human beings give another their "blood to drink"? Pregnant women nourish the fetus with their blood.

And what kind of human beings can give another their "flesh to eat"? Nursing mothers nourish their infants at their breasts. Jesus' desire that we eat his body and drink his blood seems to carry strong allusions to maternal love. It is the tender, intimate, willing nourishment of a mother that is meant by these sayings — not cannibalism, the only other literal meaning of Jesus' words. The eating of Jesus' flesh and drinking of his blood is connected in Jn 6:54–57 with an interpenetration of life. As Jesus receives life from the Father, whoever eats him draws life from him. (The image of the vine and the branches in Jn 15:1–8 is another figurative expression of the same idea.) In evoking the image of new motherhood, Jesus alludes to the closest, most intimate human relationship to tell how close he wishes his sharing of life with us to be. In all of human experience, there is no closer sharing than that between a woman and the one in her womb.

A catechesial meditation like the foregoing should not be confused with the sort of data yielded by historical–critical exegesis, or with the solid doctrine developed by theology, for different methods are employed in each instance. But such a meditation is based on clear parallels between the feminine Yahweh imagery and ordinary womanly experience on the one hand, and the eucharistic symbols on the other. As such, it rightly takes its place beside the more traditional explanations of the Eucharist in terms of sacrifice, sacrament, paschal meal, transubstantiation, and so forth. The mother imagery may be particularly effective in catechesis for first Eucharist with children.

> EMPHASIZE THE POWER OF THE EUCHARIST TO UNITE SISTERS AND BROTHERS IN CHRIST AND TO OVERCOME THE SIN OF SEXISM. UNFOLD THE EUCHARISTIC SYMBOLISM BY POINTING OUT ITS RELATION TO THE FEMININE YAHWEH IMAGERY AND TO EVERYDAY EXPERIENCES OF BOTH SEXES.

44. Matrimonial Catechesis. Homilists, catechists, and counselors must stress the equal responsibility of husband and wife in marriage. Avoid stereotypes in portraying married life. The grace of the sacrament supports the union in love and the raising of children; do not imply that it favors any one division of labor in preference to others. Both partners have authority over the children and receive their respect equally.

Catechetical materials should portray matrimony as one option among many in life. Show other kinds of family arrangements along with the nuclear family, especially the single-parent family. Allusions to marriage in the Bible, especially in Paul, need special exegesis (see #4,6,31). When applying the biblical metaphor of covenant to marriage, emphasize the elements of fidelity and love; make it clear that the marriage covenant is *unlike* the biblical suzerainty treaty insofar as the latter involved partners of unequal status and strength.

Treat divorce with compassion and realism. Never assign blame for it in a stereotypical way, for example by saying that the husband was too involved in his work and the wife spent money foolishly.

Parish programs for pre-Cana catechesis, Engaged Encounter, and the like, as well as Marriage Encounter and other catechetical programs for mature couples, need support at the diocesan and national levels. Such programs, and the materials developed for them, should reflect the spirit of these guidelines.

SHOW THAT RESPONSIBILITY FOR THE MARRIAGE, THE CHILDREN AND THE HOME RESTS EQUALLY UPON BOTH SPOUSES. TREAT DIVORCE WITH COMPASSION.

The Life of Grace

45. **The Fall.** The story of the Fall in Gen 3 gives us a fascinating mythic explanation of evil. Chapters 1 and 2 make the theological affirmation that God's creation is good. Unfortunately, much ordinary human experience contradicts that affirmation. Moreover, chapters 1 and 2 say that the sexes are created equal, but the Yahwist author knows that they are not so in real life. In chapter 3, the author explains the discrepancy. The Yahwist gives us before and after pictures, and what stands between them is an act of disobedience.

Modern readers demythologize the theology of the Yahwist when they realize that the Fall is not an event in history, but rather a state of affairs in which human being is alienated from human being — both within the person and between persons. The story in Gen 3 is a work of art, a literary work that can be interpreted validly in a variety of ways. Its meaning is virtually inexhaustible. According to one possible reading, each person is both Adam and Eve, and sin splits the self apart. In another reading, Eve stands for the generative, deliberative component of humankind while Adam represents the aggressive, active component; sin makes them work against each other. Alternatively, Eve can be all women and Adam can be all men, so that sin inaugurates the alienation of the sexes, the oppression of women, and the impoverishment of men.

The theological point of the story is that sin by men and

women is to blame for the split — not the will of God. Once that is established, the finer details of the story can be examined in perspective. We notice that, as Gen 3 tells it, the first result of the first sin is that Adam casts Eve in the stereotypical role of weak temptress and projects his guilt onto her — whereas before he had called her "bone of my bones." The second result is that Eve goes along with her new alienated status.

Is there any theological significance to the fact that the story has the serpent speaking to *Eve* when it wants to address both (v.1), while Yahweh speaks to *Adam* (v.9)? Does the story mean to say that sin comes through women? Indeed, the Yahwist probably did have some such intention, but to understand the text, the sociopolitical and religious context in which the Yahwist wrote must be taken into account. (The same sort of cultural shading is apparent in Gen 4, where the Yahwist has God reject Cain's sacrifice of vegetables and accept Abel's animal sacrifice. This is clearly a polemic against the agricultural ways of the Canaanites and their fertility rites, and a statement of support for the traditional nomadic ways of the Hebrews, who herded sheep and made animal sacrifices before they came into the Promised Land. It has no application to the relative merits of farming and herding today, of course.) Snake figures and female temple personnel who performed sacred sex were features of the rival Canaanite religion which the Yahwist was trying to combat. The differentiated punishment in 3:16–19 is not a statement of the unalterable destinies of women and men; it simply reflects the status quo at the time the story was composed. Factors like these are taken into account in an adequate exegesis of Gen 3.

Catechetical treatment of the Fall should acquaint people with the nuances of the Gen 3 story when they are able to understand the exegetical arguments. Even the youngest and simplest Christians should know that trouble comes from sin, not God, and that both men and women are guilty of sin. The connection between sin and the alienation of the sexes is clear even through the mythological language of Gen 3.

AVOID LITERALIZING THE STORY OF THE FALL. SUBORDI-
NATE THE DETAILS TO THE MAIN MESSAGE: THE SIN OF
MEN AND WOMEN CAUSES EVIL IN GENERAL AND THE
ALIENATION OF THE SEXES IN PARTICULAR.

46. **Original Sin.** The reality of original sin has been explained in different ways in the history of theology. It is both the act which Adam and Eve did in the mythical story of the Garden, and the sinful condition of the human race which everyone recognizes from experience.

The earliest Christian writers do not associate the two. However, Augustine does connect the two concepts, and introduces the idea that each generation passes original sin on to its children through what he sees as the sinful act of sexual intercourse in which the children are conceived. Anselm compares the state of "original justice" *in the Garden,* meaning a right ordering of relationships according to God's will, with the *present* state of original sin, meaning a disrupted order of relationships and a debt that human beings cannot pay off by themselves. Anselm says that Jesus pays the debt and restores the state of justice.

Aquinas and other medievals develop Anselm's juridical explanation of original sin to account for the element of deliberate choice that must be present in sin: Adam and Eve sinned deliberately, but had we been there we'd have gone along with them; now we share their punishment as we were to have shared their reward.

Modern Catholic theologians seek to preserve the insights of the tradition about original sin by expressing those insights in modern terminology. For example, original sin is seen to be transmitted to each generation not *biologically,* as Augustine had said, but *sociologically.* It comes to us because we are situated in a society that gives us bad example when it should be giving us the "grace" of good example, a society that mediates wrong values to us instead of godly values. Society was already sinful before we were born, but we "inherit" guilt for it as we personally choose to accept and perpetuate it instead of correcting it. The "original justice" of the Garden is understood to represent the will of God for us, but it is projected to the end of time as our destiny in Christ. Justification lies in our future where it summons us, and not merely in our memory of the original intention of God at the dawn of our race.

War, starvation, economic oppression, and racial hatred are all manifestations of original sin in the world today. Sexism, too, is the same kind of evil. Catechesial treatment of original sin should associate sexism with it. The following traditional descriptions of original sin apply to the sin of sexism as well. It is contrary to the original intention of God for humankind and to the destiny of humankind in Christ. It is transmitted from generation to generation. It inheres in relationships. It estranges one from God, from nature, from one's neighbor, and from one's own self. It exists before the individual is born, but individuals become guilty of it as they accept it and choose to deal in its terms. It is overcome in Christ.

CATECHESIS ABOUT ORIGINAL SIN SHOULD POINT OUT THAT SEXISM IS ONE OF THE THINGS THAT "ORIGINAL SIN" MEANS.

47. **The Struggle Today.** Christ has accomplished our justification, but we are in the in-between time when the effects of redemption are not yet fully manifested. The world and the Church continue to oppress women and men with sexist structures and expectations. Catechetical materials should portray this honestly, so that the hurt can be recognized and healed. Don't ignore the fact that people still have to struggle to live Christian lives, and that the effects of sexism and other sinful structures still thwart them. Show how life is complicated by the sexist role stereotypes which Christians must face in contemporary society. Portray the ways in which Christians resist the effects of the sin of sexism. Support people in their personal and communal struggles to overcome sexism. Don't pretend that society already actualizes the ideal of justice for the sexes. Society today is not paradise.

Children's texts should tell stories about people who try to overcome the dictates of sexist stereotypes. For instance, a little girl who feels afraid to confront a challenging situation can say to herself, "Oh, I can do that, I will do it." Or a boy who is injured can be told by his father that it is all right to cry.

PORTRAY CHRISTIANS STRUGGLING AGAINST AND BEING HURT BY THE STRUCTURES OF SEXISM.

48. **Salvation for All.** Salvation is not just "for us men." Avoid giving the impression that Jesus saves men only. Make women and girls feel that they, too, are addressed by the good news and included in God's universal salvific will. The generic term *man* does not mean the same thing as *men*. *Men* is a plural term denoting several male human beings. "Us men" sounds exclusive to women's ears; it is a phrase which should not ordinarily appear in catechetical materials or in prayers for use in a catechumenal setting.

Rather than the generic term man, try humankind, all people, all men and women, each of us, everyone, us, etc. Remember to refer to the Christian as "he or she," or "she or he." Resort to plural forms to get around the problem of gender-specific terms. Rather than, "The good Catholic helps his neighbor," say, "Good Catholics help their neighbors." Or, alternate masculine and feminine singular pronouns: "The Christian teaches his children by his own example. She speaks respectfully of her coworkers at the office." Remember that Jesus is "our brother," but we are his "brothers and sisters." Homilists should take particular care to avoid androcentric language.

EXPRESS THE UNIVERSALITY OF SALVATION THROUGH CAREFULLY BALANCING THE USE OF GENDER-SPECIFIC TERMS.

49. **Women Are Sinners.** Help girls and women to take themselves seriously as sinners. Homilists, youth ministers, catechists, ministers of adult education, and catechetical materials must distinguish society's rules from Christian imperatives. To violate the former may entail social penalties; to disobey the latter is sin. If women don't understand the difference, they cannot recognize themselves as sinners. Unless they know themselves to be sinners, there is no way for them to be saved.

Show that women bear full responsibility for their actions. Help girls form their consciences around the demands of the gospel, not the demands of social convention. Present biblical, historical, contemporary, and fictionalized stories of women who sinned, repented through the grace of God, and received forgiveness. Contrast these with stories of women who had to violate social convention to do what God wanted.

HELP WOMEN TO UNDERSTAND THE DIFFERENCE BETWEEN SINS AND VIOLATIONS OF SOCIAL CONVENTIONS. HELP WOMEN TO ACKNOWLEDGE THEIR SINS AND TO ASSUME RESPONSIBILITY FOR THEM.

50. **Women's Goodness.** Take the goodness and heroic virtue of women seriously. Saintliness is just as astonishing in women as it is in men. Do not imply that women find it easier to be good than men do, or that piety and self-sacrifice come more naturally to women. Meekness, forebearance, and the evangelical counsels are just as difficult for women as for men. Christian virtues manifested in the lives of women should not be presented as the natural, expected thing. They are a gift, a grace, and a cause for thanking God.

> CONVEY THE IDEA THAT CHRISTIAN VIRTUE MANIFESTED IN A WOMAN'S LIFE IS AN EXCEPTIONAL THING AND A REASON TO GLORIFY GOD — JUST AS IT IS IN A MAN'S LIFE.

51. **"Jesus is Lord."** This ancient statement of faith expresses the conviction that Jesus has overcome all sin, both personal and social. Sexism is among the sins that Jesus has defeated. He liberates us from structures that threaten our full humanity. His grace is the source of our courage to confront and overcome sexism in our lives and in the world. In catechetical materials, this notion should always accompany the portrayal of oppression and sexism in society.

The word *lord* in English denotes a male person. Point out that the maleness of Jesus is not essential to the Christ's victory over sin. Christ's victory is won in the lives of women as well as men. Women identify with Christ when they resist and overcome sin.

> IN DISCUSSING SEXISM, MAKE THE THEOLOGICAL POINT THAT JESUS CHRIST REALLY HAS OVERCOME IT ALONG WITH ALL OTHER SIN. THOUGH SIN REMAINS POWERFUL IN THE WORLD, THE POWER OF CHRIST IS GREATER AND GIVES US HOPE IN THE STRUGGLE.

52. **Experiences of Collaboration.** Before men and women can work together in the world and the Church, boys and girls must learn to treat one another as equals, to help one another, and to cooperate in achieving the goals of the group. They must learn to understand each other's viewpoints and to take on each other's concerns. This learning has to be experiential; it cannot come out of books.

Fostering activities and programs in which boys and girls share equally is one important tool of catechesis toward justice for the sexes. These activities, both apostolic and recreational, help form habits of cooperation between the sexes. It is not enough to have "separate but equal" sports programs, for instance. If individual teams must be segregated, then let both sexes come together in field days, in planning and attending the annual awards banquet, in earning funds for equipment, and so forth. Apostolic activities like tutoring, child care, and visiting the sick or prisoners should involve both boys and girls at every stage of planning, logistics, execution, evaluation and reflection.

The atmosphere of the religion classroom should promote egalitarian attitudes. Youth and campus ministers, CYO directors, and catechists have the responsibility to encourage a spirit of understanding and cooperation between the sexes, and to guard against tendencies to assign jobs or responsibilities according to sex. They must examine their own behavior to see whether they treat the sexes differently.

Point out that the motive for working together is the love and empowerment of Jesus, rather than the desire to please other people or to fulfill social expectations. The joy of participating in group activities with both sexes is a symbol and an anticipation of the joy of belonging to the reign of God.

What goes for youth activities goes *a fortiori* for adult activities and ministries. The equality which young people hear about in class and which they experience through their own cooperative activities must be verified in the relationships they observe among adults.

Women and men working together in a parish provide a lived expression of this equality. Catechetical teams composed of both men and women are good role models for youth and the whole parish. If such examples are not available in the parish, find some in the community (e.g., at a local hospital or campus) and invite the team to tell the parish youth about their work.

Traditional parish associations that have always been segregated by sex need to be encouraged gradually to begin joint projects. Segregated parish activities ought to be opened to both sexes. Catechetical materials should depict cooperative activities along these lines so that the experience of collaboration between the sexes can be reinforced.

> FOSTER APOSTOLIC AND RECREATIONAL ACTIVITIES IN WHICH THE SEXES CAN LEARN TO UNDERSTAND EACH OTHER AND WORK TOGETHER. DEMONSTRATE COOPERATIVE RELATIONSHIPS THROUGH TEAM MINISTRY BY BOTH SEXES AND THROUGH OTHER COOPERATIVE ADULT ACTIVITIES. DEPICT THESE RELATIONSHIPS IN CATECHETICAL METERIALS.

The Moral Life

53. **Friendship.** Portray friendship as something that everyone can enjoy with all kinds of people, because all kinds of people are worthy of esteem, respect, interest, and love. In the past, our culture favored models of friendship between men, between boys, and between boy and man. Present other models of relationships: girls who are friends and women who are friends; girls and women; girls and boys; girls and men; boys and women, and women and men. Some friendships are equal camaraderie; in others, the junior partner receives guidance and encouragement. Some friendships conform to role patterns, while others reach across the lines of age, class, race and sex in unlikely ways.

Build stories around all kinds of friendships. Find models in Scripture, history, and the contemporary Church and society. Each person is worthwhile and has something to give to others.

PORTRAY A VARIETY OF FRIENDSHIPS AMONG ADULTS
AND YOUNG PEOPLE OF BOTH SEXES.

54. **Communities.** Christian life always takes place in a community. Building community is one of the tasks of catechesis. A great variety of communities can become Christian communities through catechesis. Catechesis can even gather a community where none previously existed. The

Christian community is a place where equal nurturing and equal respect are accorded to both sexes. It is in some sense a home for which both sexes have responsibility.

The family can be a Christian community, but that doesn't mean it is the only one or the best one. Catechetical materials should represent Christian life in other communities besides the family. The workplace, the summer camp, the bowling league, the prayer group, the trade union, the chancery, the campus, the hospital — all can become places where Christians share life together. Depict men and women together in communities like these, and tell how they can help Christ to be present in them.

Religious congregations of women and of men are among the most explicit expressions of Christian community. Show that while such a community is all of one sex, the sisters and brothers pray for the whole Church, often perform their apostolic work with people of both sexes, and usually have friends of both sexes.

When portraying families, do not make every one a nuclear family. Many families in the United States have only one parent, or have other adults besides parents in the home. Many Americans, especially those whose roots are in immigrant and ethnic groups, have strong ties to a large extended family that includes third cousins and relations by marriage. Avoid role stereotyping in the home. Show women in other contexts besides the home and in other rooms of the home besides the kitchen.

Jesus, Mary, and Joseph should not be depicted as a modern Western nuclear family. The gospels mention that they had a number of relatives. Portrayals of the Holy Family should be historically authentic. It would have been impossible for three people in the small town of Nazareth in the first century to have lived in ethereal isolation from their neighbors, synagogue, and relations. Do not project stereotyped roles onto the Holy Family.

PRESENT A VARIETY OF CHRISTIAN COMMUNITIES BE-
SIDES THE FAMILY. SHOW HOW THEY COME TO BE
PLACES WHERE MEN, WOMEN, GIRLS, AND BOYS SHARE
THE LIFE OF CHRIST.

55. **The Story Beneath the Stories.** The attitudes and assumptions of the catechist, homilist, or minister come through clearly in the examples she or he chooses to make a point. Case histories that are recounted in textbooks or homilies as illustrations of moral behavior can convey unintentional messages.

Don't always start off a story with a stereotypical premise — for example, with two boys playing actively together, or with a girl sitting by herself and thinking. Such a premise has already delivered a message to the audience before the story gets off the ground. The casting of people in predictable roles bores the audience and can reinforce negative stereotypes. Jesus was a master storyteller who set up expectations in the minds of his hearers, and then shattered them by exaggerating a detail or imposing a new meaning on a popular theme. Populate stories and accompanying art with a representative number of both sexes and all ages. If the world pictured in the religion textbook is not fifty percent female, no one will believe that it is the real world.

WATCH OUT FOR THE ASSUMPTIONS, ATTITUDES, AND UNINTENTIONAL MESSAGES THAT STORY PREMISES CAN CONVEY. SHOW EQUAL NUMBERS OF MALES AND FEMALES IN CATECHETICAL MATERIALS.

56. **Responsibility for One's Life.** The choice of a career is one of the most important choices in life, because one's career sets the agenda for many of the other choices one will face. Both boys and girls will have to make career choices. Youth ministers and catechetical materials should help them understand that each person has responsibility to make something of her or his life.

One cannot choose what one does not know. Introduce young people to a range of possible careers, and to people of both sexes who have chosen them. If this cannot be done in person, rely on materials that depict all kinds of people in all kinds of jobs. (See Appendix A.) Discussions of life choices, and of responsibility for one's life, are in order. Do not imply that anyone is destined by her or his sex for any one kind of life. Encourage Christian motives in the choice of a career.

PRESENT A RANGE OF CAREER CHOICES AND SHOW THAT THEY ARE OPEN TO BOTH SEXES. POINT OUT THAT EACH YOUNG PERSON HAS THE RESPONSIBILITY AND THE POTENTIAL TO DO SOMETHING WORTHWHILE WITH HER OR HIS LIFE.

57. **Service Jobs.** Show the dignity, value, and necessity of ordinary occupations. Not everyone can be an administrator or a professional. The bricklayer and the nursing aide may be more important for the reign of God than the architect or the chief surgeon. Christians do not judge the way the world judges. Many Christians have found it easier to live out ideals of service and fellowship in an ordinary job than in a job with high prestige and high pay. Mention Jesus' teaching on the greatness of those who serve, Mt 20:25-28.

Foster esteem for the service jobs which women have traditionally held: nursing, domestic services, secretarial work, child care, and teaching. Depict men, too, in these occupations. Suggest that whatever one's job is, one can perform it in a spirit of service to the people of God.

BRING OUT THE WORTH AND DIGNITY OF ORDINARY SERVICE OCCUPATIONS, ESPECIALLY ONES THAT TRADITIONALLY BELONGED TO WOMEN.

58. **Parenthood.** The decision to have a child, which necessarily brings great responsibilities, should be made freely. Catechists, youth ministers, and catechetical materials can help to insure that the decision will be freely made by showing that marriage (and parenthood) is one possible choice among many. Women do other things besides becoming mothers; they do other things *along with* becoming mothers. Motherhood is compatible with work outside the home, although some mothers work at home as homemakers. For women, as for men, parenthood is an option not a destiny.

Portray alternative lifestyles in a way that will foster individual creative choice. Never give children the impression that the choice their own parents made falls short of the ideal. The mother who stays home is not a better Christian or a more normal women than the one who works outside the home — and vice versa. Nor is a father any less a man or a Christian if he is the parent whose full-time job is child care and homemaking.

Depict fathers taking care of children and doing housework. Occasionally portray other family members (grandfathers, aunts, big brothers) in nurturing situations. In stories and in art, explore the dimensions and possibilities of the fathering relationship as well as the mothering one. Do not give either sex a monopoly on parenthood.

SHOW THAT PARENTHOOD IS A CHOICE, NOT A NECES-
SITY FOR EITHER SEX. DEPICT A VARIETY OF PARENTING
ARRANGEMENTS.

59. **Virtues and Vices.** One traditional method for delivering moral catechesis is to describe the virtues that characterize the Christian life. Jesus uses this approach in the Sermon on the Mount (Mt 5:1-12). Moral teaching can be quite effective when it tells stories about people who practice a virtue, a work of mercy, or a beatitude. Listeners identify with the doer of the virtuous act; they enter imaginatively into the motives and decision process of the person in the story. In addition, other stories are told to illustrate faults and vices that oppose the Christian virtues.

It is essential to give both sexes models of desired behavior by illustrating each of the beatitudes, virtues, and works of mercy with stories about persons of both sexes. Both male and female figures should have parts in the stories portraying faults and vices contrary to the Christian virtues as well.

Men and women are capable of the same moral faults and the same moral strengths. Do not give the impression that either sex is excused from practicing any of the virtues. Take care, especially in art, not to imply that girls have the monopoly on virtues and boys on faults. Resist the tendency to personify restraint and self-control always in female figures, and the active-creative virtues always in male figures. Do not portray girls exclusively as the victims of aggressive acts by boys. Avoid stereotyping girls as gossips and boys as ruffians. Each sex must be helped to integrate all the Christian virtues, in imitation of Jesus Christ.

ELIMINATE SEX-ROLE STEREOTYPING FROM HYPOTHETI-
CAL CASES OF MORAL DECISION AND FROM STORIES
ILLUSTRATING THE VIRTUES.

60. **Motives and Emotions.** Make clear the difference between the imperatives of the gospel, and the demands of social role expectations and good manners. Young people encounter pressures from various quarters to conform to overlapping, conflicting patterns of behavior. Yet conformity is not the goal of catechesis. Young people need help to sort out the different pressures they feel, and to discern among them those which have moral force.

Do not present the conventional demands of society as if they were moral imperatives. Some social expectations harmonize with the gospel; for instance, it is generally true that observing basic good manners makes it easier for Christians to love one another. But neither *lady* nor *gentleman* is a synonym for *Christian*. Catechists and youth ministers are not engaged in the formation of ladies and gentlemen. Take care not to say or imply that it is just "not nice" to commit this sin or that. Lying, bullying, cheating, impurity, stealing are socially unacceptable behavior, to be sure — but that is not the only or ultimate reason why Christians avoid them.

Restrain the impulse to overreact to behaviors that are major social offences but may not be sins at all — profanity, for example. Remember that cultural factors govern what is bad language; sometimes one person's effective rhetoric is another's blue streak. Do not correct girls for what is tolerated in boys. Do not give the impression that there are "higher standards" for women.

Both sexes can show emotion in appropriate situations, and both sexes are obliged to learn self-control. Never say that big boys don't cry or that nice girls control their tempers. While the degree of emotional display deemed acceptable varies with culture, there is no reason in the gospel for it to vary with sex. Catechetical materials should attribute feelings to persons of both sexes. Stories and art can depict appropriate emotional displays by both sexes.

Catechists and youth ministers should try to discern where each person needs help in rounding out her or his personality. Many boys in our culture may need encouragement to show affection and to express their feelings of fear and inadequacy. Many girls may need encouragement to become more assertive and independent. Integration of emotions, not repression of them, is the way to a healthy emotional life. Only the healthy person succeeds at learning self–control. The Christian's motive for self–control is the love of God and neighbor, not the need to win the approval of other people.

DISTINGUISH GOSPEL IMPERATIVES FROM THE EXPECTATIONS OF SOCIETY. ENCOURAGE BOTH SEXES TO BE IN TOUCH WITH THEIR EMOTIONS.

61. **Values.** Help young people become sensitive to the difference between gospel values and worldly values. Our society esteems a man for the degree of power he possesses, his wealth, his creative achievements. Society has denied equal power, money, and chances for creative achievement to women, so they have lower status than men in the eyes of the world and often in their own eyes. There is an alternate route to self–esteem for some women: physical beauty and sycophantic behavior.

Money, power, and physical attractiveness are of secondary importance to the Christian. To pursue them for their own sake is contrary to the gospel, whether it is a man or a woman who does the pursuing. Christians esteem themselves for one reason: God sent Jesus to save us. Show young people that it is just as unchristian to despair of one's own worth because one lacks money or beauty as it is to think that one's worth lies in possessing those things. Both men and women should esteem themselves for their new status in Christ and for the works of loving service which God's grace enables them to do.

SHOW THAT THE CHRISTIAN'S SOURCE OF SELF–ESTEEM IS HIS OR HER MEMBERSHIP IN CHRIST RATHER THAN WHATEVER ATTRACTIVENESS, TALENT, WEALTH, OR ACHIEVEMENTS HE OR SHE MAY HAVE.

62. **Sins of Women.** Both sexes are capable of all sins. Pride, anger, covetousness, lust, envy, gluttony, and sloth are abstract, general categories of sin, but opportunities for committing them present themselves in situations that are all too particular and concrete. Our culture provides somewhat different occasions of sin for men and for women. Moreover, it perpetrates the lie that some particular sinful acts are natural to the sex that commits them. In women, the culture condones vanity, gossip, backbiting, inactivity, and preoccupation with appearance. It condones competitiveness, drunkenness, arrogance, insensitivity, and prodigality in men. Thus, the culture helps persuade men and women to sin in characteristically different ways.

Catechesis, however, cannot tolerate such a double standard. The gospel brings to light the manifestations of sin in the lives of both men and women. Point out and criticize both the masculine and the feminine versions of the "capital sins." Sex is no excuse for condoning any shade of these in anyone. Alert young people to the particular forms in which they will encounter temptations to these sins.

> BE SENSITIVE TO THE MASCULINE AND FEMININE FORMS
> THAT TEMPTATION TAKES. LET THE LIGHT OF THE
> GOSPEL ILLUMINATE ALL VARIETIES OF SIN FOR WHAT
> THEY ARE.

63. **"Your Neighbor's Wife."** Place this sexist phrase in its historical sociocultural context. In the Hebrew Scriptures the law always takes the male point of view and virtually all the legislation uses androcentric language (see #30). The tradition of the male viewpoint continued in Church legislation, which is not only androcentric but in places overtly misogynistic in tone, content, and intent. These facts should be presented honestly. Help women to understand that in the law God addresses them as well as men.

The prohibition of adultery in Ex 20:14 applies equally to men and to women. Theoretically, the punishment is the same for both — death (cf. Lv 20:10; Dt 22:23–24). However, the actual practice may have been less severe, at least in the case of the men. Aquinas taught that adultery was a worse sin for a woman than for a man, because she violated property rights in making it possible for a bastard to become her husband's heir. (This is only one example of how the legal treatment of women has been confused with property law.) Jesus' words to the woman taken in adultery provide a corrective to this pathological development in moral theology.

Catechesis should emphasize equal sexual responsibility for both sexes. The Christian goes out of his or her way to consider the weakness of the other person and the harm that could come to the other because of one's own actions. Modesty, prudence, and the other safeguards to purity are responsibilities for both sexes.

> EXPLAIN THE ANDROCENTRIC VIEWPOINT OF BIBLICAL AND CHURCH LAW, BUT MAKE IT CLEAR THAT BOTH SEXES HAVE EQUAL RESPONSIBILITY FOR SEXUAL MORALITY.

64. **The Sin of Sexism.** There is a moral responsibility for all Christians to resist the sin of sexism in society and to pray for liberation from it. All must undergo conversion from sexism in understanding themselves and one another. Homilists, counselors, catechists, and youth ministers should promote conversion away from sexism and support efforts to break down sexist social structures.

> PRESENT THE MORAL OBLIGATION TO RESIST SEXISM. SUPPORT PEOPLE WHO ARE UNDERGOING CONVERSION FROM THE SIN OF SEXISM.

65. **Historical Accuracy.** If individuals and the Church itself are to be converted from the sin of sexism, they must first know about it. Honestly portray the history of oppression of women by the Church along with the oppression of women in society. This oppression had repercussions for men, too, because it impoverished and repressed them as well. This historical background helps to explain why sexist structures linger in the Church and in society today. But an explanation is not an excuse. Loyalty to the institutional Church requires that loyalty to the gospel come first. Mention that the Church in its fidelity to the gospel is trying to set right its historical injustices to women.

HONESTLY DESCRIBE THE HISTORICAL AND PRESENT-DAY INJUSTICES OF THE CHURCH AGAINST WOMEN.

66. **Feedback.** When stereotyped attitudes or assumptions about the sexes appear in students' papers, art, projects, or reports, take care to point them out. They are not mistakes, but they are elements discordant with the gospel which should be raised to consciousness and criticized. Catechists and other ministers can listen for sexist attitudes in the conversation of the people with whom they work. Both sexes are liable to harbor sexist assumptions. There is a duty to correct such attitudes, gently and at the proper time and place. Where attitudes are concerned, change should be gradual but steady.

CORRECT SEXIST ATTITUDES, ASSUMPTIONS, AND STEREOTYPES IN THE CONVERSATIONS, ART, AND COMPOSITIONS OF THOSE BEING CATECHIZED.

Mary and the Saints

67. **Exceptional People.** Many women and men have followed Christ so closely that their lives provide examples for Christians today. Tell the stories of historical and contemporary women who became saints by overcoming the sexist expectations of their times. Mention the social, cultural, political, and economic conditions in which they lived. Also tell the stories of men who followed Christ by stepping outside of the sexist stereotypes of their time and place.

Some saints underwent virtual martyrdom because of the sexist structures of their society. Therese of Lisieux is a good example. In the original copy of her autobiography, she tells of her vocation to the priesthood and of her sorrow because as a woman she could not be ordained. She asked God not to let her live beyond the age when men received the sacrament of orders, for fear she could not bear the disappointment. Yet these facts, so central to Therese's identity, were deleted from the published version of the autobiography.

Explain the canonization process. Women have never had a say in selecting saints for canonization or in setting the criteria for selection. All canonized women saints, therefore, exemplify the values of the men who selected them. Not all saints are canonized. Encourage young people to recognize saintliness in the women and men whom they know, and in themselves.

Saints are not simply objects of admiration; they disclose to us the potential in our own lives.

TELL THE STORIES OF MEN AND WOMEN WHO IMITATED CHRIST BY OVERCOMING THE SEXIST EXPECTATIONS OF SOCIETY.

68. **How They Did It.** Show that saints follow Christ through fidelity to their own inner awareness of their identity and purpose. They get in touch with a depth dimension of reality beneath the structures of the social world; they encounter God and their own true selves there. In this way they find the courage to violate the norms of the group when it is necessary. Catechists and youth ministers should encourage students to imagine how this must happen. Dramatization and role-playing are good techniques for this. Encourage quiet reflection as well. Suggest that the young people will go through a similar process themselves when they make important choices in their lives, such as the choice of a career or a state of life. One finds one's own identity through the steady, faithful practice of prayer and through ruthless honesty with oneself. God's grace gives us the power to swim against the cultural current when that current flows counter to gospel values. While it is the community which introduces us to God, ultimately God speaks to us in the depths of our own heart and we obey God there.

POINT OUT THAT THE SAINTS FIND GOD'S GRACE AND THEIR OWN IDENTITY BY GETTING IN TOUCH WITH A DEPTH DIMENSION OF REALITY BENEATH THE SOCIAL FABRIC OF THE EVERYDAY WORLD

69. **Saints for Each Season.** The use of saints as models is an appealing catechetical technique for people at every stage of development beyond early childhood. Different models attract people at different stages of development. Young people have to learn to conform to the demands of the community before they can responsibly transcend them. People about the ages of 10-13 are beginning to understand what it means to belong to a group, a community. They are particularly receptive to models who personify the ideals and values of the group, and with whom they can identify. For this age group, present conforming saints of both sexes — those who worked for the good of the Christian community and received its love and approval. Describe also the personal weaknesses of such saints and tell how the community helped them.

Older adolescents and young adults can understand the nonconforming saints who encountered opposition not only from the world but from the Church as well. Portray the struggle of men and women whose fidelity to God led them to disappoint the expectations of even the good people in their own communities. Point out that the saints continued to show charity toward those who misunderstood them, and continued to listen to criticism of their actions from those in authority. Some saints decided to bear injustice for the sake of peace in the community; others chose to denounce and overthrow injustice. Both options show courage and charity.

More mature people may respond to the example of saints who showed perseverance and fidelity. Some of these were victims who turned their situations into creative opportunities; others were people in positions of responsibility and power who carried out their duties with heroic love and great wisdom.

CONSIDER THE DEVELOPMENTAL LEVEL OF THE AUDI-ENCE WHEN SELECTING SAINTS FOR CATECHETICAL EXAMPLES.

70. **Variety.** Choose saints from a broad range of life-styles, social classes, and ethnic groups. Portray a variety of virtues in saints of each sex. Saints are saints because they resemble Jesus Christ. Avoid stereotyping male and female saints. Present saints of each sex in equal numbers. Elizabeth Seton, John Neumann, Martin de Porres, and Frances Cabrini deserve special attention.

REPRESENT BOTH SEXES AND ALL SOCIAL GROUPS AMONG THE SAINTS WHOSE STORIES ARE TOLD IN CATECHESIS.

71. "Confessors and Holy Virgins." The traditional Catholic literary genre known as "lives of the saints" has some special sexist stereotypes all its own. The Roman Martyrology was notorious for its androcentric viewpoint and misogyny. The hierarchical arrangement of the calendar of saints used to classify women by marital status. A woman could be a virgin martyr, a virgin not a martyr, a widow, or a holy woman. In a few years it may become possible to speak humorously of these old classifications and of the sexist tales in the Roman Martyrology. Today, however, it is still necessary to work at rooting out the impressions they have left in the minds of the Catholic population. Take care not to let the old stereotypes get into today's materials and programs.

> COUNTER THE EFFECTS OF THE SEXIST STEREOTYPING IN
> TRADITIONAL LIVES OF THE SAINTS BY PRESENTING FAIR
> AND HISTORICALLY ACCURATE STORIES OF MALE AND
> FEMALE SAINTS.

72. Collaborators. Tell the stories of men and women saints who worked together for the good of the Church. Show that they mutually inspired and encouraged one another. Show how they made up for one another's inadequacies and strengthened each other. Explore the character of the relationship of each pair, and compare the relationships to demonstrate their variety. Point out that these men and women went beyond the vision of their contemporaries. Here is list of some partner saints:

> Paula and Jerome
> Teresa of Avila and John of the Cross
> Scholastica and Benedict
> Clare and Francis of Assisi
> Louise de Marillac and Vincent de Paul
> Jane Frances de Chantal and Francis de Sales.

> PROVIDE EXAMPLES OF MALE AND FEMALE SAINTS WHO
> WORKED TOGETHER FOR THE CHURCH.

73. Mary. The Bible gives us very few biographical facts about Mary. Everything catechesis says about her must be based on the scriptural account of her life. Liberate the teaching potential of the figure of Mary from the traditional stereotypical presentation of her. She is a woman through whom God confounds the role expectations of the leaders in her society. Show her to be a person who clearly understands herself and her place before God. She is a woman of great faith, deep prayer, utter trust. Her "yes" to the angel's message makes redemption possible. Explore and meditate upon the sentiments she expresses at the Annunciation, in the Magnificat, at Cana, and through her silent courage at the foot of the cross. Just as the Christ is a figure whom both sexes imitate, Mary gives an example for both men and women to follow.

The mariological dogmas of the Immaculate Conception and the Assumption tell us more than that Mary is a special person. They have implications for every woman and every man in the Church. The Immaculate Conception demonstrates Christ's power over sin and the reality of the new creation brought about through our redemption. The Assumption anticipates what will happen to the bodies of all those who are born again in Christ. Catechesis should emphasize these meanings and avoid putting Mary on a pedestal where she becomes irrelevant.

Besides the biblical account of Mary's life, there is another source for catechesis about Mary: the traditional devotions by which people in the Church have honored the Mother of God and reflected on her role. Explain these devotions with reference to the culture in which they originated. For instance, Mary as Our Lady of Guadaloupe becomes intelligible when the history of the conquest of the Aztecs is presented and Mayan iconography and mythology are explained. Understanding the historical context makes it possible to understand what the devotion means to say about the Mother of God and about Christ. Remember that all Marian devotions point to Christ.

FOLLOW THE SCRIPTURAL EVIDENCE IN PRESENTING MARY AS A WOMEN OF FAITH WHOSE EXAMPLE CAN BE IMITATED BY BOTH MEN AND WOMEN.

Death, Judgment, Eternity

74. **Stewardship.** At death each man and each woman answers to God for the use he or she has made of the abilities, the time, and the material resources which God gave to him or her. Women and men alike have the serious obligation to develop their potential and to work for the coming of the reign of God. Jesus' parable of the talents traditionally has been interpreted as a warning about the coming judgment (Mt 25:14-30, Lk 19:11-27; cf. Lk 12:48 and 13:6-9). Catechesis should point out that the warning is meant for both sexes.

EXPLAIN THAT MEN AND WOMEN WILL FACE JUDGMENT
ACCORDING TO HOW THEY HAVE USED THEIR TALENTS
FOR THE REIGN OF GOD.

75. **"For I Was Imprisoned."** Matthew makes it clear that we will be judged according to what we do to alleviate the bodily and spiritual suffering of the neighbor (25:31-46). The sexist structures of our society and our culture cause great harm to men and women who are our neighbors. Working to liberate them from the effects of sexism is working to liberate Christ. Point out that a good way to help neighbors in need is to work for the eradication of the effects of sexism.

> IT IS CHRIST WHO IS IMPRISONED AND MADE A STRANGER BY SEXISM. POINT OUT THAT THOSE WHO DO NOT TRY TO ALLEVIATE THE MENTAL AND PHYSICAL SUFFERING OF THEIR NEIGHBORS HAVE NO SHARE IN THE REIGN OF GOD.

76. **"Neither Male nor Female."** After we rise from the dead we will live a new and wonderful kind of life. Little is known about what that life will be like. We do know that the bodies in which we rise will be our own bodies, for we expect personal identity to continue. However, Jesus tells the Sadducees that there will be no more marriage beyond the grave (Mt 22:23–33; Mk 12:18–27).

We can get some idea about the quality of that new risen life for men and women if we examine its beginnings on *this* side of the grave. The life which Christians share in baptism is an anticipation of the risen life. Paul tells us that for those baptized in Christ the distinction between male and female is overcome (Gal 3:27–28). Today when we experience equality of status in the Christian community, collaboration between women and men for the realm of God, and sharing of life at the eucharistic table among brothers and sisters, we are experiencing something of what the risen life will be like.

Whereas the Genesis creation accounts describe an original equality of the sexes that is disrupted by sin, Paul says that Christ defeats sin and inaugurates a new creation where equality between the sexes is restored.

> SHOW THAT CHRISTIANS ARE DESTINED FOR UNITY WITH CHRIST IN A RISEN LIFE THAT OVERCOMES ALL DIS-TINCTIONS BETWEEN PEOPLE.

Other Concerns

77. **Art.** Pictures in children's textbooks capture the imaginations of young readers and can deliver more persuasive messages than do the stories they illustrate. It is important to keep the artwork free of stereotypes and negative portrayals of the sexes. Pay particular attention to the art and the captions in children's activity books.

Male and female figures should be comparable in size, numbers, activities, importance, attractiveness, attitude, stance, centrality of placement, and so forth. Where historical accuracy requires an all-male picture, complement it nearby with a predominantly female picture of equal importance. Illustrate scenes where there would normally be a mixed group of people; for example, the congregation at Mass or the crowds following Jesus.

Dress should be realistic. People at work wear appropriate work clothes. Women do not always wear dresses. Girls engaged in active play would wear jeans and T-shirts or jackets, the same as boys. Customs of dress in the United States vary in different sections of the country and among different ethnic groups. Let illustrations reflect the variety of customs among people in the Church, both in worshiping situations and in other everyday contexts.

AIM FOR A BALANCED AND REALISTIC REPRESENTATION
OF BOTH SEXES IN ART.

78. **Auxiliary Materials.** All instructional materials used in catechesis should reflect the spirit of these guidelines. Posters, charts, videotapes, films, slides, records, cassette tapes, and overhead transparencies are included. In each medium there is a grammar of image and sound that can carry messages on several levels. Each must be free of stereotyping and negative portrayals of the sexes. This rule holds regardless of the source of the material, whether it be produced by a national publishing house, a diocesan office, a local committee, or an individual catechist.

With more mature groups, it is of course permissible to view a sexist film or to listen to a sexist record album for the purpose of discussing the content and criticizing its sexist elements.

TAKE CARE TO ELIMINATE SEXIST ELEMENTS FROM
AUDIOVISUAL MATERIALS.

79. **Dramatics and Activities.** Catechists and youth ministers are responsible for seeing that no sexist message is conveyed in any of the activities employed in catechesis or in other ministerial work. These include arts, crafts, dramatics, mime, dance, role-playing, simulation or instructional games, music, and story-telling.

Be particularly careful in selecting plays and musical productions that will be presented publicly. These not only demand intense personal imaginative involvement of the participants, but they convey their messages to the whole community as well and can do great harm if they portray the sexes in stereotypical ways. Choose dramatic vehicles that present positive images of the sexes and that critique sexist injustices in society.

In Christmas pageants, do not cast the girls exclusively as angels and the boys as shepherds. If there is a May procession, a boy may be selected to crown the statue of Mary. Avoid sexist stereotyping in games. Experiment with role-playing to help the boys understand the girls' perspective, and vice versa.

DRAMATICS AND OTHER ACTIVITIES MUST NOT PERPET-
UATE SEXIST STEREOTYPES.

80. **Social Events.** Sports programs, dances, proms, bingos, car washes, fashion shows, bake sales, picnics, and so on must foster positive relationships of equality between the sexes. Encourage the group to reflect on how they plan and execute these events and to suggest ways that would better express the gospel ideal of justice for the sexes. Both sexes should participate in as many of the affairs as possible. Equal support should be given the boys' sports teams and the girls' teams. If there is a queen of the prom, there should be a king of the prom, and criteria for selection should be comparable. If the group has elected representatives, help it to critique the decision process by which the leaders are chosen. If the president is always male and the social chairperson is always female, ask the group why.

BRING SOCIAL EVENTS INTO ALIGNMENT WITH THE GOSPEL IDEAL OF JUSTICE FOR THE SEXES BY ENCOURAGING GROUPS TO REFLECT ON HOW THEY FUNCTION.

81. **Teachers' Manuals.** Notes for catechists should encourage them in their own conversion away from sexism and help them raise their consciousness of this sin. Call the catechist's attention to the positive images of the sexes in the textbook. Point out that the catechist's own attitude and interpretation determine the effectiveness of catechesis toward justice for the sexes. Alert catechists to opportunities to catechize against sexism. Sensitize them to sexist images in magazines, books, movies, and other mass media so that they in turn can help students recognize and interpret these.

EXPLAIN THE TEXTBOOK'S APPROACH TO JUSTICE FOR THE SEXES AND POINT OUT ITS BALANCED REPRESENTATION OF MEN AND WOMEN. INVITE CATECHISTS TO BRING THEIR OWN ATTITUDES AND PRACTICES INTO ALIGNMENT WITH THESE.

82. **Notes for Parents.** Call parents' attention to the positive images of the sexes and the critiques of sexism presented in their children's books. Explain how these things are connected to the gospel message. Ask parents to think about the significance of catechesis toward justice for the

sexes, and to support it. Suggest that they periodically discuss it
with their children and reinforce its message.

EXPLAIN TO PARENTS THE CONNECTION BETWEEN THE
GOSPEL AND JUSTICE FOR THE SEXES. ENLIST PARENTS IN
THE EFFORT TO ACHIEVE THIS GOAL THROUGH CATE-
CHESIS.

83. Selecting Catechists and Youth Ministers. The
catechist is the most important human element in
catechesis. Persons who are chosen for this ministry should
already have demonstrated their sensitivity to the sin of sexism,
especially to its manifestations in language and its inroads upon
the Christian symbol system itself. Youth ministers, too,
instruct young people in Christian living, values, and symbols,
although they do so outside the classroom setting. This task
demands that youth ministers also sensitize themselves to the
manifestations of sexism. The character and attitudes of the
catechist or youth minister act as a model for young people.

Dioceses must provide for the continuing formation of youth
ministers and catechists. Among other things, this means
supporting their spiritual growth and heightening their
awareness of sexism and their competence to deal with it.
Parishes must encourage and support the emerging roles of the
catechist and the youth minister. Both men and women are
suited for these jobs and should be recruited for them.

CHOOSE MEN AND WOMEN WHO ARE AWARE OF THE SIN
OF SEXISM TO BE CATECHISTS AND YOUTH MINISTERS.
FOSTER THEIR CONVERSION FROM THIS SIN IN PRO-
GRAMS OF CONTINUING FORMATION.

84. Policies. Administrative policies can convey a sexist
message that contradicts the gospel. There must be
career development and advancement channels for religion
teachers, catechists, youth ministers, and ministers of adult
education. These channels must be open equally to both sexes
and to lay, religious, and clerical personnel. Parish youth
ministers are to devote equal time and resources to both sexes,
seeking to integrate boys and girls, young men and young
women, into the total life of the parish.

Participation in programs should be equal for both sexes, so that no sexist message is inadvertently transmitted. Dioceses with all-girl and all-boy high schools should take care that both kinds of institutions have equal facilities and equal funding. Where, in the past, financial and intellectual resources have been concentrated in seminaries for the theological training of men alone, steps must be taken to facilitate the higher education of women in religious studies so that they, too, can prepare for ministries in the Church.

ADMINISTRATIVE POLICIES, ESPECIALLY THOSE AFFECT-
ING THE PROFESSIONAL PREPARATION AND ADVANCE-
MENT OF CATECHISTS AND OTHER MINISTERS, SHOULD
REFLECT THE GOAL OF JUSTICE FOR THE SEXES.

85. **Mass Media.** One objective of catechesis toward justice for the sexes is to enable people to recognize the sexist images, assumptions, and attitudes that are propagated in the secular mass communications media. These media include books, magazines, newspapers, records, tapes, radio, television, and films. Each of these media carries content of various kinds: drama, fiction, news, ballads, advertisements, and so on. People remain vulnerable to the messages these convey unless they can bring those messages to explicit consciousness and critique them. Students should also understand the institutional processes by which mass-mediated messages are produced. There are points in the processes where pressure for change is particularly effective. Christians should apply pressure there to encourage production of more positive images of the sexes.

HELP PEOPLE DEVELOP THE ABILITY TO CRITIQUE THE
IMPLICIT SEXIST MESSAGES CARRIED BY THE MEDIA OF
MASS COMMUNICATIONS.